"A cutting-edge pioneer in the field of business coaching, Dr. Otazo knows—and speaks—the truth about how to get and keep the job you want. Regardless of your age or stage of your career, you'll find practical tips and tools to make your workplace journey smoother, more enjoyable, and potentially more profitable. *The Truth about Managing Your Career* is a must-have for your career library."

—Lois P. Frankel, Ph.D., author of Nice Girls Don't Get the Corner Office and Nice Girls Don't Get Rich

"Two points stand out in this clear and cogent book: 'Work is a game.' And, 'It's worth playing well.' Dr. Otazo, a consummate corporate insider and outsider, sums up the standing knowledge of excellent gamespersonship in this succinct manual for people entering the workforce, and for people standing back to gain better perspective on their own careers."

—Art Kleiner, editor of strategy+business, author of Who Really Matters: The Core Group Theory of Power, Privilege and Success

"Dr. Otazo distills years of her wisdom, insight, and global coaching expertise into each of her '5-minute chapters.' The result is a collection of highly polished gems to be contemplated at the many crossroads of your career journey."

—Saj-nicole A. Joni, author of The Third Opinion

"Dr. Otazo has created a roadmap to successful career management. This book provides invaluable advice for every stage of business life laying out clear, concise, and practical solutions for the working professional. Read either in part or in its entirety, an essential tool for business success!"

—Valerie Foundoukis, Vice President, Global Organizational Development Head of Strategic Coaching Practice Credit Suisse, New York

"Years of browsing in airport bookshops have made me highly skeptical of the management 'wisdom' we are fed today. However, here at last is a book that leaders will instantly recognize as making real practical sense—I wish I'd read it 25 years earlier."

—Ritchie Bent, Group Head of Human Resources,
Jardine Matheson Ltd

"This book should be subtitled 'Everything you need to know to succeed in the real world of business but were smart enough to realize that if you asked, the people around you might perceive it as weakness!' If you let it, *The Truth about Managing Your Career* will be your bible, coach, best friend, and secret weapon as you propel your business, career, or project to the next level."

—Michael Neill, creator of www.geniuscatalyst.com
and author of You Can Have What You Want
and The Seven Myths of Success *audio programs*

"I feel lucky that Dr. Otazo has coached me through many a career challenge. Now her years of insight and experience are open to readers of this indispensable guide. For anyone making for the heady summits of organizational life, like oxygen they should have it on hand for regular intake."

—Julia Rowntree, author of Balancing Act:
Art and the Business of Survival

"Dr. Otazo beautifully succeeds in distilling more than two decades of supremely practical organizational know-how in this gem of a book. Her style is clear, concise, and immediately accessible. She speaks to the mind and emotions simultaneously and galvanizes action. Reading this book and applying its pragmatic wisdom will assure your safe passage through many contemporary corporate minefields."

—*James Flaherty, Executive Coach, author of* **Coaching: Evoking Excellence in Others**

"*The Truth about Managing Your Career* is easy to use, succinct, and wise. Dr. Otazo provides lots of useful tips for performers in the theatre of organizational life. But her book's greatest strength is in showing why a career should be built on principles. A key principle is respect for others, senior and junior, even when you don't agree with their views. Another is earning trust through honesty, compassion, and clarity. Especially if you work in a large, hierarchical organization, you should read, re-read, and always have at hand this great book."

—*Gerard Fairtlough, Founder /CEO of biotechnology company Celltech and author of* **The Three Ways of Getting Things Done: Hierarchy, Heterarchy and Responsible Autonomy in Organizations** *and co-author of* **The Power of the Tale: Storytelling in Organizations**

"A real gem. As a managing director in a large global company, I have seen first-hand Dr. Otazo's practical advice and insight really making a difference. Each self-contained chapter contains helpful tips that will give the reader the opportunity to take control of their career and to focus on the key issues that face today's workforce."

—*David Buckley, London, UK*

"This is an amazing book! The intensity and sincerity come through because the words and experience Dr. Otazo imparts are true to the core. I did not want the book to end. It delivers sage advice that makes me think about what I will do tomorrow and priceless perspective on what I did just yesterday!"

—Douglas Hofmeister, Partner, Accenture, LLP

"I only wish I had had Dr. Otazo's advice when I started in corporate life. Even now, as an independent, I will be drawing on the tips in her book as I work with a great variety of people around the world."

—Barbara Heinzen, author of **Feeling for Stones: Learning & Invention When Facing the Unknown**

"I have long admired Dr. Otazo's work as a coach. This is a great practical guide for coaches and our clients alike. Thank you, Karen, for sharing your insights and experience with us."

—Ellen Kumata, Partner, Cambria Consulting; Practice Leader, Cambria Coaching

"The Truth? I've worked with Dr. Otazo for many years and she has always been a wise counsel with an uncanny ability to get to the heart of any issue, and her proposed solutions invariably work. Her latest book encompasses the wisdom and insights gained from more than twenty years of working with and coaching executives across a wide range of industries and cultures. A copy of *Truth* will be highly recommended reading for my Leadership team and will be freely available for all employees who are committed to and want to learn the truth about career development."

—Milton Steele, Vice President & Group Manager, FMC Corporation

THE TRUTH
ABOUT MANAGING
YOUR CAREER

THE TRUTH ABOUT MANAGING YOUR CAREER ...AND NOTHING BUT THE TRUTH

Dr. Karen L. Otazo

PEARSON
Prentice
Hall

An Imprint of Pearson Education
Upper Saddle River, NJ • New York • London • San Francisco • Toronto
Sydney • Tokyo • Singapore • Hong Kong • Cape Town • Madrid
Paris • Milan • Munich • Amsterdam

Vice President and Editor-in-Chief: Tim Moore
Acquisitions Editor: Paula Sinnott
Editorial Assistant: Susie Abraham
Development Editor: Russ Hall
Associate Editor-in-Chief and Director of Marketing: Amy Neidlinger
Cover Designer: Sandra Schroeder
Managing Editor: Gina Kanouse
Senior Project Editor: Lori Lyons
Copy Editor: Gayle Johnson
Senior Compositor: Gloria Schurick
Manufacturing Buyer: Dan Uhrig

© 2006 by Pearson Education, Inc.
Publishing as Prentice Hall
Upper Saddle River, New Jersey 07458

Prentice Hall offers excellent discounts on this book when ordered in quantity for bulk purchases or special sales. For more information, please contact U.S. Corporate and Government Sales, 1-800-382-3419, corpsales@pearsontechgroup.com. For sales outside the U.S., please contact International Sales, 1-317-581-3793, international@pearsontechgroup.com.

Company and product names mentioned herein are the trademarks or registered trademarks of their respective owners.

Printed in the United States of America

First Printing, January 2006

Pearson Education LTD.
Pearson Education Australia PTY, Limited.
Pearson Education Singapore, Pte. Ltd.
Pearson Education North Asia, Ltd.
Pearson Education Canada, Ltd.
Pearson Educatión de Mexico, S.A. de C.V.
Pearson Education—Japan
Pearson Education Malaysia, Pte. Ltd.

Library of Congress Cataloging-in-Publication Data

Otazo, Karen L.
  The truth about managing your career : --and nothing but the truth / Karen L. Otazo.
    p. cm.
  Includes bibliographical references.
  ISBN 0-13-187336-9
  1. Vocational guidance. I. Title.
  HF5381.O922 2006
  650.1--dc22

                        2005018362

To Napier Collyns, with gratitude for the insight and inspiration for this book and many others to come.

CONTENTS

Contents

Contents

Contents

PREFACE

Don't read this book. Skim it. Scan it. Find what you need right now and use it. Then come back later when your needs change.

The 60 straight-to-the-point Truths work in any order. Each one is a coaching session chock-full of tips for succeeding in business with confidence and finesse.

I have spent more than 20 years coaching executives on three continents and in all manner of organizations, ranging from major conglomerates and media firms to charities and nonprofits. And I have learned that common factors consistently pave the road to career advancement wherever you work and whatever you do. One major constant is that you need to manage your career proactively. When you picked up this book, you rose to the challenge.

The Truth About Managing Your Career will work for you at any stage. If you are just starting out, it introduces you to professional life and how organizations work. If you are well into your career, questioning where you are going and what you want, this book can help you find the path or organizational niche that's right for you and your talents. If you are already advanced on the career ladder, this book can help you climb higher. If you are at a crossroads, this book will help you rethink your career. And if you are advising and coaching others, it will give you clear, concise, and instantly useful information on the key issues you need to cover.

Each 5-minute Truth focuses on one business truth and illustrates why it's important to your career. Practical advice, illustrated by real-life stories, shows you how to apply each truth to your working life.

Think of this book as your atlas. Wherever you are on your career path, you can use the tips and truths on these pages to get where you're going. This book points out hazards that could slow your progress or even run you off the road. And it guides you toward the fastest, clearest routes. Let this book be your road map to low-stress success. Enjoy the trip!

Karen Otazo

Karen Otazo

ACKNOWLEDGMENTS

I would like to thank the following people for their support and contributions to this book. FT Pearson/ Prentice Hall: Tim Moore, Paula Sinnott, Russ Hall, and Lori Lyons. Colleagues and friends: Pat Di Franco, Lois Frankel, Jean Horstman, Michael Neill, Colleen O'Brien; and my husband, from whom I've learned so much. My thinking partner: Daisy Froud.

About the Author

Dr. Karen L. Otazo is a global executive coach and thinking partner for multinational companies worldwide. With more than 25 years working experience with clients in the U.S., China, India, Indonesia, Hong Kong, the UK, Europe, and Singapore, Karen is uniquely equipped to work with executives in global corporations, joint ventures, and strategic alliances. Her blue-chip client list includes organizations as varied as investment banks, consulting firms, NGOs, and conglomerates worldwide. She is a fellow of the Society for Organizational Learning, a past chair of the Boston University Roundtable, and on the advisory committee of the Business Arts Forum of the London International Festival of Theatre.

PART I

THE TRUTH ABOUT STARTING A NEW JOB

TRUTH 1

HITTING THE GROUND RUNNING CAN GET YOU INTO TROUBLE

It's common when starting a new job to be told that you need to "hit the ground running." Experienced people who appear in the job market after their companies have downsized often hear this. The expectation is that since they bring connections, experience, and other intangible assets to a new job, they don't need time to learn the new culture and the players. The temptation on hearing this is to dive in with all your energy, ready to make an amazing first impression. After all, you do need to prove yourself. Although your boss may be satisfied, that attitude can get you into trouble in more ways than one.

The main problem with hitting the ground running is that you don't know what you're running into. Will your actions make waves among your new coworkers, will you rock the company boat in general, or will you even, in your eagerness, perform in a way that will have long-term disadvantages you can't see at first? By the time you do, it can be too late. As a newcomer to the role, you are put in a vulnerable position where you lack foreknowledge of the situation and must rely on your bosses to tell you what needs doing. However, there is no guarantee that they have this fully figured out. People see a situation from their own vantage point and may be unintentionally blind to other perspectives. You now have the dilemma of how to make a good first impression yet not step on toes.

Senior management may see the situation from a dollars-and-cents viewpoint and not understand what's happening on the ground. That's what happened to Leroy. He was an experienced oil field manager when he was asked to come in and save money on an offshore operation. He came into the job and immediately found big cost savings by substituting work boats for helicopters to get the workers to and from oil rigs offshore. What he didn't do is take the time to check on how the old hands would react to the change. They saw the change as a loss of almost two days of their "week off" time with their families since they worked week on/week off. They were so furious that they staged a work slowdown action and called in a union. The result was a backlash and bad publicity that could have been prevented by a bit of groundwork.

Before you dive in, no matter what the pressure, it pays to take time to do the groundwork—to carefully read the files and review the situation by talking with people. You are unlikely to get the chance again. You have to ask for the perspective of others, not just that of your boss.

Far from impressing your coworkers, coming into a job at a fast pace can actually upset them. Employees on assembly lines who worked too fast were called "rate busters," and factory managers hate the repercussions from the reaction to them. You may be far from a factory, but you can still upset people by pushing too hard and too fast without getting buy-in. Colleagues may fear that you will show them up by making them appear slow in comparison. You can also miss out on chances to tap into their thinking about the project. Without early collaboration, it will be hard to get their buy-in and support later on. There are few organizations where it is possible to get things done as an individual contributor beyond the lowest levels of the hierarchy.

More often than not, "hit the ground running" is a piece of corporate-speak masking hidden flaws in the company. Be particularly wary if the phrase is accompanied by requests to "get in there and fix things" or "clean things up." Such terms hint that something is lacking organizationally. If your job is in a state where there is no time for preparation, it is likely that other things are being done in a similarly scattershot way. It may be that the company is looking to you for a quick fix, which is not a good position for you to be in (unless you are hired for that reason). "Fixers" become expendable when the dirty work is done and are easy scapegoats if things don't improve. If you really are entering an emergency, you should be paid a premium, as any turnaround artist would be.

Unless you're a time-limited consultant or interim manager, no matter how much you're expected to fix things, always put aside time to get feedback and guidance from others and think about the long term as you start a job. Those first months are crucial for getting up to speed and for creating a lasting partnership with coworkers, subordinates, and others.

TRUTH 2

ACT DUMB AND THINK DIRTY: THE LESS YOU SAY, THE MORE YOU LEARN

Kids growing up in tough neighborhoods quickly learn to "act dumb and think dirty." Mouthing off might make an older, tougher kid think you're a "wise guy." So you keep your mouth shut ("act dumb") and trust no one ("think dirty"). In the meantime, you watch and listen, checking out how others behave, testing their integrity, working out how you fit into the mix.

Such tactics serve adults equally well in any new organizational neighborhood. The less you say when you start a job, the better you position yourself to learn about the organization and how it works, and your new colleagues and how they work together. The early days should be about listening and observing while giving away as little as possible. After all, you don't know who's who or what's what.

The early days should be about listening and observing while giving away as little as possible.

Acting dumb doesn't mean being sullen or reticent so that

people think you are shy or rude, but it does mean not volunteering opinions or information unless asked and, when you *are* asked, keeping your response to a minimum. You don't want to shoot your mouth off and then find out you've trampled on someone's sacred cow about how business should be conducted. So take part in day-to-day easy conversation, but keep your ideas to yourself.

It's a good idea to have some pat answers to standard questions worked out, like where you came from and how you like working in the new company. But keep these short and sweet: the kind of 30-second "elevator speeches" you might offer a stranger between floors. You don't want to reveal a lot about yourself until you are comfortable with your coworkers and their way of thinking. Once you've given your answer, you can politely ask the other person questions about how things are done "around here," building your knowledge of how the company operates.

Now, what about "thinking dirty?" You may think this sounds a bit paranoid. Well, don't! See it as maximizing your opportunities. In those early days, you have the privilege of checking out your coworkers and thinking about how to work with them in the best possible way. You need to be prepared to think the worst, particularly of those with whom you will have to work closely. Take advantage of being the silent person in the room to observe and listen to your colleagues in different circumstances. Then actively process and question the "data" you collect. This intelligence-gathering will help you know who you can trust and will help you prepare strategies for dealing with those about whom you're not so sure.

There are key things to look out for. Do your colleagues badmouth people who are not in the room? If so, be aware that they might do that to you. Do they reveal things about the business that are confidential? If they do, it's possible that they'll let your own thoughts and ideas slip. Do they change what they say with different people? If so, it may be hard to know if what they tell you is the whole story or just the part they want you to hear.

"Act dumb and think dirty" is a savvy tactic to protect yourself at work. It's useful not only when you start a new job, but also on a daily basis. Bring it into play whenever you need time to figure out a new situation.

TRUTH 3

HAVING MADE THE MOVE, YOU SHOULD GROW WHERE YOU'RE PLANTED

When transplanting a seedling or shrub, any good gardener knows that the immediate "after period" is critical. The act of moving can send even the hardiest plant into shock, with disturbed roots taking time to adapt to new soil. Humans can be similarly affected by a move. Wherever we work, we put down roots in the form of habits, customs, and relationships. The longer we stay in one place, the more embedded we get. When we pull ourselves up to move to a new job, it can prove tricky to acclimate to a new environment.

The key to a successful move is to fully engage with where you've been replanted. You need to let go of your old workplace and its way of doing things and put down roots in your new organization by showing loyalty and appreciation. Unless asked, it's not a good idea to even mention your old company. It's often tempting to compare a new place to former experiences, especially if that place is particularly well known, or if you had a particularly good time there. However, doing this publicly can lead to trouble.

Wally, a project manager, was used to going to his boss to deal with interdepartmental conflict. When he started a new job, he was aghast that, among other things, this was no longer the case. On a daily basis he would say "At AT&T, my boss used to say…" or "At AT&T we did it this way" to his new colleagues. Not only could he not help comparing, he also thought that if he dropped enough hints, his coworkers might start doing things differently. That didn't happen! At first, individual colleagues were just irritated. Soon they were laughing behind his back. Although eventually Wally settled into the new company culture, developing strong relationships with both boss and colleagues, his initial behavior considerably slowed down his integration by creating unnecessary friction.

A new workplace will want your skills and experience, but they won't want to be compared to past employers, however important these were to your formation. This is not just about avoiding outright critical comparison. Implied criticism, such as amazement at the inefficiency of the IT system, or mentioning how motivating it was that your former employer paid for an annual training week, will provoke as negative a reaction.

Don't compare your new workplace to your past employers.

Your intention may be to make helpful suggestions, but they will not be heard as such. New arrivals have to earn the right to critique by showing that they understand the organization.

Your new coworkers will be watching to see how well you settle in. Success in a former job doesn't mean that you will automatically flourish. No matter how well you know your stuff, there can be clashes with a new organization's norms and values. For example, Joyce moved from an Anglo-Dutch company with a consensus culture to an American company with an entrepreneurial one. She continued to expect that every decision would require checking with all concerned parties, no matter how long that took. Joyce's intent was good, but her colleagues saw her conscientious behavior as time-wasting, or worse, obstructionist. It took some honest feedback from others to set Joyce on the right path. Now she relishes the freedom to act that her new position offers.

Rather than looking to your own past, take the time to find out about the past and ethos of your new organization. Talk to people who've done your job before you, asking how things came to be. You don't have to repeat history—just respect it. This can also give you leverage. For example, if you can cite how the company has cared about people's development in the past, you can show that it makes sense to uphold these values by offering you training in the present.

New arrivals have to earn the right to critique by showing that they understand the organization.

You prove that you're a member of your new company with loyalty and support for your new colleagues. Rather than fretting about the loss of your supportive boss or efficient systems, take a positive perspective and focus on appreciating what *does* work. Then, once you've paid your dues, you can devote your energies to making things even better, working with others rather than against them.

TRUTH 4

TAKE OWNERSHIP OF YOUR JOB WITHOUT STEPPING ON TOES

Forty years ago Robert Ardrey, writing about the "territorial imperative," amazed readers by showing that humans are no less territorial than animals when it comes to staking out our "turf." We may not bite strangers, urinate on streetlamps, or tunefully sing our claims to territory (particularly not in the office), but we do want others to be clear on who we are, what we know, and where our influence lies.

When starting a new job, it's important that you seek out and claim your "territory": the tasks, issues, and decisions you are responsible for and the way in which you do them. However, in proving yourself, you must take care not to step on anyone's toes. This is a time for establishing working relationships with others, not making enemies. In your new job, everyone else will have been there longer than you, and they will have their own views about how things should be done. You need to find a balance between showing them respect and convincing them to cede control to you so that you can make your mark.

A key first step is to get a sense of the organizational culture—the various collective habits that make up the way in which the company operates—and work to fit in with it. Do people chat while they are working, or not? Do they go out to lunch, or do they eat at their desks? Do they visit others when they have a question, or send an e-mail? When you notice how all these little things are done and follow

A key first step is to get a sense of the organizational culture.

suit, you are less disruptive as a newcomer and less likely to provoke resentment.

Fill your calendar with meetings and conversations when you're new, engaging as many people as possible. Don't expect others to come to you. Introduce yourself, and ask them questions about their roles and opinions on important matters. But wait until you have something concrete to discuss before you ask for time with very busy people so that they don't feel you are wasting their time.

Some toes are more sensitive than others. There are two groups of people around whom you should tread particularly carefully. The first is people who in any way consider your work part of their territory, such as the person who held your job, or who worked up the project, before your arrival. The second group is those directly below you in the hierarchy, who may feel that they know more than you, and maybe even have wanted your job. In both cases, make initial communication as neutral as possible. Ask these people open-ended questions, resisting the temptation to offer your opinion unless asked. Treat them and their opinions with respect. Respecting an opinion does not mean that you have to follow it. You just need to take it into account.

Resist the temptation to offer your opinion unless asked.

As a newcomer, you should always start from what is already there. Before you change things, listen to others and be gracious. No matter how much of an expert you are, and even if you've been brought in for your talents, you still need to make sure that you keep others in the loop and respect their ways of doing things.

TRUTH 5

IT'S IMPORTANT TO KNOW WHO KNOWS WHAT: BUILD YOUR CIRCLE OF INFORMATION

Once upon a time, if you needed information, you usually knew where to go for it. If no one in your company could help, a paid professional would. Information was in the hands of a few experts, such as lawyers, librarians, and financial advisors, with clear titles and knowledge fields. They offered ready-made solutions for most information needs.

In today's "information age," information is available from multiple sources. The few trusted experts have become a smorgasbord of options. There is more specialization. One legal expert is no longer enough for every legal question, and one big consultancy firm can't help with all organizational matters. With less emphasis on degrees and titles, and more on real-life experience, it has become harder to quickly assess people's knowledge. And knowledge is accessible in new ways—via the Internet, e-mail, or phone—making the location of advisors less important. Getting the right information despite (or even because of) the range of information available can be confusing and time-consuming.

That's where a good "circle of information" comes in: a diverse group of people, contacts gathered over time, who know your thinking and who are there when you need them. You can rely on them to give it to you straight, whether you need to find a new employee, learn how to do business with a new culture, or leverage your brand. You can also learn from your circle by working through ideas, plans, and problems with them.

It's important to have information sources both inside and outside your organization. When you need to keep things low-key, an outsider may be a better bet, since insiders can unintentionally reveal things to others. You should also ensure that you have a few trusted "thinking partners"—not just family and friends likely to agree with you, but people who will challenge you and ask you questions. They don't need to be experts as long as they understand you and your business.

It's important to have information sources both inside and outside your organization.

Thus, you have your inner circle and an outer or working circle. The former consists of a few people you can wholly trust, who get to hear your innermost thoughts. Members need to show loyalty while having no fear of questioning you. Your working circle is wider, made up of all the people, inside and outside your company, including experts, who you can call on for information or help with knotty issues. Its membership fluctuates; you bring in the right people for the situation you're in.

You build your circle of information by asking around your network for recommendations, checking people's backgrounds and experience using the Internet, and then bringing useful folks on board. Test them either by involving them in a small project or by making use of the initial free access that often comes with a referral to ask some questions of a professional over the phone. Once you find good people, professionals or not, nurture these relationships by using them regularly, honoring their guidance, and keeping them informed. You may want to use them when you aren't desperate for help so that they take your call when you are. However, beware of using the same people all the time, or you may find yourself depending on someone too much or thinking purely from one perspective.

You need to vet your circle of information all the time to confirm that people are still right for you. Ask yourself whether members respond to you in a timely manner and make an effort to keep you in the know. Do they offer personalized responses that show they have taken the time to understand your situation? Do others still respect their thinking? Last but not least, are they committed to keeping confidential information confidential and loyal enough not to talk about you behind your back? If an expert talks about you on the ski slopes of Switzerland, the information may find its way to your competitor in New York. We live in a small world with an active Internet!

TRUTH 6

RECOGNIZING WHOM TO TRUST KEEPS YOU FROM GETTING BURNED

When you start a new job, as with any new relationship, there is a period of trust-building. Your colleagues need to develop trust in you, as you do in them, if your working relationships are to be effective. This reciprocity is essential in the workplace; however efficient you are, you can't do your job in isolation. If you can't trust your colleagues to be there for you, you could end up in big trouble.

There is no formula for generating trust. Trust is above all a feeling, something that gradually evolves through shared experiences. However, it can be helpful, in building effective working relationships, to carefully consider what kind of trust you need in whom. For example, you require a very different kind of trust in a clerk or assistant than you do in a colleague with whom you are working on a controversial new idea.

There are four major types of trust to think about as you work with others:

- **Get-it-done trust** involves knowing that others will meet commitments on time and within budget and that they will alert you to any potential delay. This is particularly vital with assistants or with anyone to whom you delegate tasks. You test this kind of trust by making small requests and noting how and when people get them done. Then you'll know who you can trust when a crucial project with an inflexible deadline comes along. You can nurture a climate of get-it-done trust by making it clear that people should come to you with any concerns about meeting deadlines as soon as they have them.

- **Expertise trust** is about believing in someone's special knowledge or ability. It's a vital kind of trust to have with any experts you work with. You must be certain that their advice is sound and their knowledge current. For example, when hiring a consultant to advise on a Hong Kong joint venture, you should check that his or her experience postdates the colony's handover to China, or it will be of limited use. You need to know that experts will give you the real scoop and the whole scoop whenever you ask or, ideally, even before. You test expertise trust by double-checking with others the information you are given until you feel fully confident in someone.

- **Political savvy trust** comes from knowing that your colleagues understand workplace norms and how to play the organizational game. It is bound up with confidentiality and discretion and is important in any colleague with whom you work strategically. Being great at getting things done, or being an expert in his or her field, is no guarantee that a colleague deserves political savvy trust. Your brainstorming colleague with great off-the-wall ideas may not realize the importance of keeping these ideas low-profile until you have warmed up your boss, and he might let something slip that halts your plans. Political savvy trust gradually builds with time as you observe how colleagues behave in others' company.

- **Structural trust** is needed whenever you work with someone from elsewhere in your company. Ideally, it comes from knowing that the other person puts the organization's interests before his or her own and gives credit to other departments rather than taking total ownership. Given that resources are usually stretched, and that different departmental interests often don't coincide, developing total structural trust is tricky. However, you can generate a good working trust by establishing clear frameworks in advance, rather than taking blind leaps of faith. If you have to split a commission with someone on another team, for example, you should agree on the percentage split before you team up to approach a customer.

Every occasion for dealing with others, however low-key, is a chance to test their trustworthiness. If someone breaks your trust once, you should certainly be wary of asking for his or her support with anything important in the future. There's not much time and space in organizational life for second chances.

PART II

THE TRUTH
ABOUT WORKING
WITH BOSSES

TRUTH 7

HONOR YOUR BOSS:
IT PAYS TO ADJUST TO THE WAY YOUR
BOSS LIKES TO DO THINGS

In some countries, employees may subordinate their own profile to that of their boss. They strive to help their bosses look good, and may even do their work, or speak on their behalf, to help them out of tricky situations. Such practices might seem alien, even inappropriate, in the typical American office. Yet a good relationship with your boss makes all the difference to your career potential. If your boss believes that you have his or her best interests at heart, he or she will be more committed to helping you succeed.

All good relationships take work. Maybe you are one of the lucky ones, blessed with great boss-employee communication, synching perfectly in thinking and working styles. However, it is more likely that your working relationship has its share of gripes and misunderstandings. You'd like more direction, you'd like less, you'd like to be listened to, you'd like your boss to understand what you are saying. So what do you do?

It's tempting to assume that your boss should spot when things aren't working. After all, it is his or her job to manage you. Remember, though, that your immediate manager is likely to have more than one subordinate and won't change his or her habits just for you. You, in contrast, have only one or perhaps two bosses and can invest effort in adapting to their needs. Honoring your boss is about going out of your way to find what works for him, rather than expecting him to figure out how to work with you. If you can subtly effect a change for the better, your boss will notice the improvement and think more highly of you. And in a large organization, an appreciative boss is the conduit for news of your talent and success to travel up the hierarchy.

Jean, working in Asia, reported to a boss halfway around the world who seemed to concentrate all her attention on people close by. So each week Jean called his boss to talk things through with her. To his frustration, despite these efforts, his boss never quite remembered what they had discussed, no matter how often information was repeated.

Then Jean tried a new tactic. He drew up a discussion sheet of key issues and found a reason to visit headquarters more often, armed with this list. With the sheet before her, the boss suddenly got much "smarter." She would carefully go through the items one by one, considering the information and clearly taking Jean's ideas on board. Jean now uses the "cheat" sheet" with his boss both in person and on the telephone. She now thinks that Jean is smarter and more reliable and views him as a loyal and trusted member of staff.

Different people take in information in different ways. Most executives, like Jean's boss, prefer reading or seeing information to hearing it. If an approach doesn't work once, determine how your boss would like to be informed rather than trying more of the same. A written list, a plotted chart, or a verbal debriefing? Regular updates or just a review at the end? Either ask her directly or just observe her habits—whatever you feel more comfortable with.

Communication may be a two-way process, but one party can do much to alter the dynamics. It is in your best interest to take the lead, strategically but subtly, in communication with your boss. Your actions can pay dividends. Not only does honoring your boss's way of doing things build a more efficient working relationship, serving you both in the day-to-day processes of business, but your boss will understand it as an expression of your loyalty and commitment. He or she will then be more likely to protect and reward you for this behavior if times get lean or tough in the organization.

TRUTH 8

YOUR BOSS CAN MAKE (OR BREAK) YOUR REPUTATION

When you feel you deserve a raise, when you need to resolve a conflict, or when you are ready for a promotion, who do you call on first? Whether you like it or not, it's your boss.

In all but the smallest organizations, the person directly above you in the hierarchy has more influence over your career progression than anyone else, however much you nurture relationships with influential figures higher up. Your boss conducts your yearly review, assessing how you perform against targets. He or she also helps decide your bonus or raise. Less officially, your boss talks with lots of other people in the organization, in places where you are not. You need to make sure that your boss talks positively about you wherever and whenever possible.

Clearly, the better your boss knows you, the better he or she can represent your value and potential to others. Make sure that your boss has good things to say at the ready by arranging regular career conversations, formal or informal, to keep him or her well informed about your achievements, your concerns, and the challenges you are facing.

A boss can help you out with more than just good stuff. When trouble comes along, a supportive boss can be your trump card. In a conflict with peers, for example, around issues such as office space or commission sharing, a supportive boss will act as a referee, even as your emissary, to alleviate tension and resolve issues. Even if you don't end up with the outcome you wanted, or if things turn sour, a supportive boss can confirm that you tried to work things out, keeping your reputation intact.

This is all very well if you have a good rapport with your boss, but it's more challenging if you don't. If your boss feels affronted by or actively dislikes you, he or she will not speak well of you and might even make you look bad in public. It's vital that you not acquire the reputation of a "problem" employee by virtue of what your boss is saying. So tread carefully, looking for opportunities to build support. Whenever you have the chance, it pays to say good things about your boss to others and to acknowledge what he or she has done for you, such as "My boss really opened doors for me on this one."

Whatever you think about your boss, the trick is to always behave respectfully.

You nurture reciprocal mutual support by what you say. Reinforce desired behavior by showing your boss loads of public respect when he or she treats you well, for example, but behave in a neutral manner when the opposite happens. Whenever possible, thank him or her for any support shown, however minor. Whatever you think about your boss, the trick is to always behave respectfully and look for ways to make him or her feel good about your relationship.

Your boss's usefulness depends to some extent on how much others respect him or her. You get a sense of how well a boss is thought of by tapping into the office grapevine and by observing who is in your boss's network. If you feel that his or her word is not listened to, you might want to build relationships with others at your boss's level—by asking their opinions on key projects, for example. They may then speak well of you and your initiative to others.

The quality of the boss-employee relationship is the number one reason worldwide that people either enjoy their jobs or feel the need to change them. Pay daily attention to strengthening that bond whenever you can, working to develop a relationship of mutual trust and support.

TRUTH 9

KISS THE RING: HIERARCHY MATTERS

Someone once asked a Washington insider how to deal with important people you can't stand. His reply: "You put on your respectful face, and you don't blink." This strategy is known in business circles as "kissing the ring." Its origins lie in a much earlier era, when royalty and clerics wore rings of office denoting their status. Bowing your head as you kissed their rings was how you showed respect for their office while not necessarily feeling that sentiment toward the characters themselves.

Why go to the trouble to show deference to someone you don't like or respect? In the cut-and-thrust world of business, as in the political sphere, it's all about survival. Or, to look at it more positively, enlightened self-interest. Like it or not, the business world is structured by a strong sense of hierarchy. Why else would we be so fixated on gaining promotions and better titles? Those high up can have a significant impact on your reputation and career: positive if they like you and see you playing by the rules, or negative if they feel slighted by you in some way. Showing them the appropriate respect helps keep your career path obstacle-free.

Why go to the trouble to show deference to someone you don't like or respect?

"Kissing the ring" might mean responding in a neutral-to-positive way when someone important says something off-base in a meeting. Or staying positive with your boss when he or she doesn't understand what you're trying to do or say. However irritated or amazed you feel, keep your facial expression kind and free of negativity, a kind of poker face. It's worth practicing this in front of a mirror so that you're ready to put it on when you need it.

"Kissing the ring" isn't about sycophancy. It's simply about respecting the senior person's position and the responsibility that goes with it, while also understanding that senior egos are as sensitive as anyone else's. There's nothing wrong in principle with telling a senior person that there might be a better way of doing things, but make sure that you think strategically and don't react there and then, especially if others are present. If you are genuinely concerned about something, you might want to bring it up in private in a neutral way but not make a big deal out of it. You do this by talking about it in a low-key manner, tactfully introducing your point by saying, "By the way, what do you think of..." or "Can a case be made for the other point of view?"

Are there "don't kiss the ring" moments, too? You bet. As soon as anything looks the slightest bit immoral or illegal, you need to stop and think. Don't jump to conclusions, but once you've confirmed that something improper is up, do everything you can to extricate yourself from the situation before you get into trouble. For example, if your company requires the highest-level person at a dinner to pick up the tab, you might well want to hesitate when asked to pay for something so that your boss doesn't have to put it on his or her expense report. Illegality is something you should always report, without exception. Some ex-employees of Enron or HealthSouth, currently in jail, probably wish they had spoken up, or even left their jobs, rather than keeping mum.

"Kissing the ring" is one of a repertoire of respectful behaviors that will keep you in good stead with high-ranking people. In the military you might call it "saluting the stripes." At some point in your career you will have to suck in your gut and show deference to a senior person you can't stand. Be prepared for it.

TRUTH 10

YOU CAN LEARN A LOT FROM DEALING WITH A BAD BOSS

Ever had a bad boss? If the answer is yes, consider yourself lucky. Believe it or not, you learn a great deal from having to deal with a bad boss for a short period of time. However, that's the key: short periods. While long stretches will grind you down, a stint of a year or less can function like a corporate boot camp, equipping you with an arsenal of tools for dealing with future bad behavior from bosses, colleagues, and others. It can even help you become a better boss yourself, not only by giving you the experience of managing tricky characters at close range, but by giving you a clear sense of behaviors to avoid once you are in charge.

Having a bad boss can help you become a better boss yourself.

Bad bosses come in all shapes and sizes. While the very worst have nasty temper tantrums, change their minds at the drop of a hat, or stonewall your every effort, there are plenty of others who are just a bit irritating, unsupportive, or manipulative. Rather than let them waste your time and sap your energy, use their bad habits as training exercises to hone your people management skills. Here are three of the most common boss faults and ways you can put them to work for you:

Delegating at the last minute: When you are well organized, nothing is more annoying than when your boss suddenly dumps a load of stuff on your desk that needs to be done by tomorrow. Especially if you had plans for the evening.

Action: Rather than complaining or muttering under your breath, start to proactively manage your boss's delegation by showing a regular interest in what priority projects he or she has coming up. You can then volunteer to begin working on some of that stuff right away. Not only does this reduce nasty surprises by keeping you ahead of the game, it also makes your boss see you as someone who is looking out for his or her interests.

Micromanaging: Some bosses seem to be constantly on your back, incapable of letting you get on with your work. This can irritate you by coming across as a lack of trust.

Action: Don't take this behavior to heart. Instead, think of a control-freak boss as someone who just needs to see the details to feel secure. You can play to this need in ways that put you in control. Start keeping a checklist of all current tasks to address, check off, and add to every time you talk with your boss. You might also ask your boss to designate high, medium, and low priorities, directing your energies to the high ones first. Your boss will bother you less once you articulate this detail in advance together, confident that he or she knows what you are busy doing, freeing you to do things your way some of the time.

It's your responsibility to adjust to how your boss likes to do things, not the other way around.

Wanting everything done his or her way: Sometimes a boss insists on a very different approach to work from the one that suits you. The differences in preferred style can cause tension, confusion, and long-term relationship problems.

Action: The challenge here is to grin and bear it and adapt to circumstances, however irritating they are. As the subordinate, it's your responsibility to adjust to how your boss likes to do things, shortcomings and all, not the other way around. So, for example, if your boss likes to see issues in writing, take the time to write them down, even if you prefer to talk things over. In doing so, you can take pleasure and pride in developing and honing valuable skills of flexing and adapting. These will serve you well in other situations, helping you work and communicate well with people of many different styles and habits. And in the short term, your boss will see you as smarter and more efficient.

PART III

THE TRUTH ABOUT WORKING WITH OTHERS

TRUTH 11

THRIFTY EXECUTIVES KEEP GOODWILL ACCOUNTS FULL

In the 1950s, American supermarkets created loyalty plans involving the award of green stamps with each purchase. You pasted the stamps into special books, redeeming them later for prizes. Even after the stamp system was replaced, people would joke about "gaining and using up green stamps" in interpersonal relationships. You gained stamps by supporting people or giving them what they needed and used them up when you behaved badly toward them or asked for special favors.

Such transactions go on all the time in the workplace. Savings methods have evolved, however, and today we're more likely to refer to goodwill bank accounts when describing relationships. Accounts with colleagues are healthy when they are happy with how you treat them, and they gradually empty as you strain or test a relationship. Wise executives keep their accounts in the black, not just with peers and bosses, but with assistants too. These people often go unnoticed and unthanked, but they can make all the difference when you need something to happen. Goodwill accounts are not, however, *quid pro quo* (something for something). The deposits you make are investments in your future.

You create deposits in goodwill accounts every day by showing real interest in others' contributions. This means listening to them, asking questions, supporting them, and honoring their actions, even with a simple thank-you. Since information is an important commodity at work, you can fill up your goodwill account with someone, including a subordinate, by keeping him or her in the know about people and events. You can even deposit goodwill by asking for guidance from someone who enjoys giving it. Socializing—spending time with good food and drink—is also often an easy way to generate goodwill savings.

You create goodwill by showing real interest in others' contributions.

Some deposits are bigger than others. Their size depends on the worth of what you do in the other person's eyes. Large deposits come from giving a colleague a heads-up that keeps him or her out of trouble, or from opening the right doors to give someone access to an important person inside or outside the company. Taking responsibility for something you didn't do or saving someone else from blame may even earn you enough goodwill to secure a promotion or plum assignment. But think of the disciplinary consequences before you do this!

Conversely, you make withdrawals from goodwill accounts when you request favors, information, support, or extra funding or time on projects. Again, the size of the withdrawal is consistent with how much the issue matters to the other person or people. Making someone look bad in front of others can result in a very large withdrawal. For some people, any questioning or push back is an immediate withdrawal. For others these are a routine part of doing business. So treat others carefully until you have gauged enough about them to understand how they feel about these behaviors. You should also be extra careful when you are under stress: a carefully maintained account can quickly be emptied by just a few short words or angry reactions. In the heat of the moment you may not even realize that you are behaving inappropriately, but others will.

Aspiring executives keep their goodwill bank accounts filled up for whenever they need to make a withdrawal. It's just good business sense.

TRUTH 12

APPRECIATING DIVERSITY INCREASES OTHERS' APPRECIATION OF YOU

It's fascinating how much habits learned during childhood endure into adult life, profoundly affecting how we see the world. During our early years, our minds construct embedded mental models of how things should be. These models are so strong that, even after spending many years in a country in which the steering wheel is on the other side of the car, most Americans would still have to think twice about which seat they need to use as a passenger!

Mental models come into play every time we meet someone or do something new. I recall watching a panel discussion with an American head of diversity. He felt that one of the participants, a woman from the Middle East, wasn't committed to the topic because she wasn't passionate enough. What the diversity executive needed to learn is that the American mental model of commitment—energetic enthusiasm—is not necessarily true for all cultures and groups, Arab women among them.

Most companies today declare a commitment to diversity, eager to ensure that employees from all backgrounds are understood and respected. But how many people, having filed away the policy, really know what appreciating diversity means? The truth is that it is not just about including others because that's the politically correct thing to do, but about realizing that others act, communicate, and think in

How many people really know what appreciating diversity means?

different ways than you, and that understanding and nurturing those differences will bring added value to your work.

The greater the range of ideas and opinions you can generate, the better the collective brain will work, as colleagues spark off each other and learn from each other's differences. Paying attention to colleagues' favored ways of working and communicating, individual or cultural, rather than trying to force your style on them, will result in not only a happier team but also higher productivity. And those are the things that prove to bosses that you really are in charge of the situation and are worthy of their respect.

Take Fred's story. Fred works in Kuala Lumpur for a major U.S. company. A few years ago, he noticed that his Malaysian employees often talked animatedly among themselves and clearly had interesting ideas but rarely spoke at meetings. Fred looked for the reason. With the help of a local colleague, he discovered that the Malaysians found it hard to express themselves well in English without preparation and felt uncomfortable jockeying for airspace with the fluent Americans.

So Fred created a system that would work for everyone, American and Malaysian. Ideas were to be collected from people well before each meeting in order to draw up a shared agenda that all personnel were ready to speak about. From that point on, conversation flowed at meetings, and the team flourished. Fred's initiative not only led to better teamwork, but the impressive results also raised his profile at U.S. headquarters.

Fred was working across cultures, but his attitude would be equally effective in an all-American office. The key rule is never to assume that others will present their thinking, or respond to circumstances, in the same way as you. Forcing them to do so only causes discomfort and dulls motivation. Rather than equating lack of participation with lack of initiative, ask your colleagues if your approach works for them, or ask them how they like to receive information. Make accommodations for differences by setting ground rules to ensure that the concerns and contributions of all colleagues are solicited and acknowledged.

At the same time, you should never assume that because someone is from a different country or culture, he or she will automatically behave differently. There's nothing more excruciating than watching someone speak English very slowly to a visitor from abroad, only for that person to respond in fluent English. The ideal stance is to be open to someone's needs or differences but never to approach him or her with preconceived expectations.

Working for a large organization means managing communication across all kinds of barriers and among a diverse range of personalities. Inclusion is about working to ensure that you get the best from everyone. That's not just about following policy, but about stepping back from your own mental models and treating all colleagues with the same generosity and understanding you would like to receive.

TRUTH 13

GOOD LISTENING MEANS TUNING IN TO YOUR SPEAKER

"If we were meant to talk more than we listen, we would have been given two mouths and one ear." You may have heard this saying, or others like it, as a child. It's equally important advice for an adult at work. "He doesn't listen" is one of the most common complaints about colleagues and bosses. And when you don't listen, people think you don't care.

> **"He doesn't listen" is one of the most common complaints about colleagues and bosses.**

Now, perhaps you *do* care; it's just that you're not great at concentrating on what others are saying. Or perhaps you're sure that you *do* listen. However, the key is not what you do, but how your actions are perceived—whether others *think* you are listening. There are many reasons why others may think you're not listening, ranging from your eye contact to the way you use your body to the manner in which you respond verbally.

The good news is that whether or not you were born a good listener, you can employ techniques to become a better one in others' eyes. Listening techniques are all about "tuning in." This means being fully present as someone is speaking and not doing anything else. It may help to think of yourself as a radio dial, tuning yourself to the other person's station so that you hear him or her clearly and without interference. If you tune in like this, and display the signs of doing so, to whoever is addressing you, others will appreciate that you are making the effort to understand them.

It's important to move away from distractions when it's time to listen to someone. We are bombarded with all kinds of competition to listening these days, from deadlines to the Internet to the telephone. Relaxing your body by ensuring that you are comfortable also helps open "tune-in space" in your brain. So does maintaining eye contact. Imagine that your face is a satellite dish moving to face the speaker. Listeners can nod to reassure others that they're listening, but speakers tend to look to your face for reassurance, so remember to give them eye contact.

Tuning in takes different forms in different people. Some tune in by "seeing" what they hear and may need to look off into space in order to listen. Others need to do something with their body, such as wiggling their foot, tapping their pencil, or doodling. If you are one of these people, it's important to let others know that you are staring into space or drawing not because you are bored but because it helps you concentrate on what they are saying.

How you respond to the speaker is further evidence of how well you have been listening. Too quick a response may make people feel that you aren't thinking about what they said. However, waiting 3 seconds after someone finishes gives you time to tune in to her words, and also shows that you weren't just waiting for a pause so that you could speak. Repeating some of the speaker's words and ideas back to him and asking clarifying questions are also indicators of a "tuned-in" listener.

To really listen, you must tune in with more than your ears, tune out distractions, and let others know, through words or actions, that you're following what they're saying.

TRUTH 14

CRITICISM WORKS BEST WHEN IT'S COMPASSIONATE

Dale Carnegie's *How to Win Friends and Influence People* was first published in 1936 and is still in print, many decades and 15 million copies later. How's that for a best seller? One of Carnegie's best lessons stressed the importance of making people feel important and appreciated, even when you are asking them to change what they do.

Criticism is part of working life. We all have to get it and give it, whether officially through appraisals or informally from bosses on a daily basis. However, we welcome it to varying degrees. If you think about your own experiences with receiving criticism, the times when you have taken it best were probably occasions when someone appeared to have your best interests at heart. You emerged from the discussion with a positive sense of what you needed to do next. This type of feedback can be summed up as "compassionate criticism." Carnegie was a master of it.

Carnegie shows how to help someone change by encouraging him or her to see a situation objectively, rather than through the filter of personal feelings. You achieve this by assuming a position of impartiality yourself, behaving not as negative critic but as positive mediator, helping the person realize the difference between inadequate old behaviors and promising new ones for him- or herself. Describing current behavior in words that are free of anger or judgment allows you to steer people toward other ways of thinking or working without causing offense or resentment.

The first stage in delivering compassionate criticism is careful observation. Before saying anything, devote some time to thinking about how to describe the other's behavior in a neutral way. It can be helpful to think of your eyes and ears as a television camera, objectively recording the person's actions. Next, describe what you see to the person, offering a second picture alongside what might work better, so that the gap between the current and improved behavior is evident.

The first stage in delivering compassionate criticism is careful observation.

Giving an example of a time when the person demonstrated the desired behavior is often helpful. It brings a positive to the criticism and shows your belief in him or her.

The final stage is to discuss together how to close that gap, focusing on creating a new picture going forward rather than reflecting on the negative. For example, when talking to someone who tends to do things at the last minute, you might say, "When you try to wing it, you tend to come across as nervous. However, I've observed that when you take time to prepare, you do a good job with your presentations. Even if you don't always have time to practice the whole thing, have you thought about just practicing the beginning and ending several times?"

A new picture is the key to compassionate criticism. Psychologists have shown that if you tell people not to think about pink elephants, that is all they will think about! However, if you then ask them to think about, say, red sports cars, they immediately stop thinking about elephants, because there is another picture in their minds. Likewise, in the workplace, if you tell people to stop doing something, their instinctive reaction, emotionally and psychologically, is to take a defensive position. They either continue doing the same things or they focus so hard on not doing them that their behavior may appear uncomfortable or contrived. It's essential to substitute a new picture to provoke positive change.

TRUTH 15

PROMPTNESS MATTERS: BEGIN AND END MEETINGS ON TIME

A middle-aged Chinese executive is due at a meeting in Beijing. Delayed by a traffic jam, he repeatedly looks at his watch. Finally, he jumps out of his taxi and runs the last few blocks, dodging pedestrians, cars, and bikes. When he arrives at the meeting, sweaty and disheveled, he is horrified to see that he is 3 minutes late. Apologizing profusely, he takes his seat.

The meaning of "punctuality" differs enormously in different parts of the world. For this businessman it was a requirement to be at his meeting on the dot. For most Americans, it would be perfectly acceptable to be 5 or 10 minutes late. Nevertheless, wherever we are in the world, thinking in terms of the scheduled time for meetings is a key part of effective performance.

Meetings are important units of time in organizational life. Unless there's an unavoidable delay or obstacle, the general expectation is that meetings will begin and end on time. Anything else can send a message that someone's time isn't really important.

Now, you may think you're pretty much on time to meetings. But ask yourself: If a meeting is scheduled for 2 p.m., do you aim to be there right at 2 p.m., or do you arrive a bit early, calm and composed, ready for the meeting? There's a difference. If you always try to cut it close, there's more likelihood that something will get in the way, and you'll actually be late. Being even 5 minutes late not only causes you to miss out on important information, but it also makes you less able to participate. At the worst, you'll feel stressed and flustered, and at best you'll have no chance to settle yourself and get your thinking ready to be at your best. Being any later than 10 or 15 minutes can be interpreted as a sign of disrespect, or even a power play. So resist the temptation to answer one more phone call or check your e-mail before you leave the office, however busy you are!

When you are the person running the meeting, you have not only the responsibility, but also the power, to start and end on schedule. Don't be kind to others by letting them come in late. Starting on time shows that you are a professional and that you and the meeting matter. At the beginning, you can state when the meeting will end and that it will have a "hard" finish, which means on the dot. No matter how great the conversation, ending a meeting on time is just plain efficient; it focuses minds and allows people to keep other commitments. If there is truly more to review, the discussion can continue offline, on e-mail, or at the next meeting. If it is vital that you continue that day, you should indicate, in advance, that extra time is possible. If you find that you get lost in the discussion, arrange for someone to knock on the door with 5 minutes left to remind you to wind up the meeting.

Ending a meeting on time focuses minds and allows people to keep other commitments.

Beginning and ending meetings on time is an easy and public way to help shape your reputation as a reliable and in-control professional. Being on time to attend meetings, or being a bit early, is the best way to shine as an attendee. Don't miss the opportunity.

TRUTH 16

CONFIDENTIALITY COUNTS

"Loose lips sink ships" said an Allied slogan during World War II. It reminded nonmilitary citizens and members of the armed forces alike that one casual comment could have critical consequences. Keeping quiet was the only way to ensure that information did not fall into enemy hands. Something mentioned to a friend or acquaintance could be passed to someone else less friendly who might employ that information to dangerous ends. The safest option was to say nothing.

We may not be in a conflict situation at work, and the impact of letting something slip may not be so disastrous, but a similar attitude toward the dissemination of information is nevertheless advisable. The dealings of organizational life result in much confidential information, only some of which you will be party to. Keeping quiet about what you know helps protect your company, the individuals who work there, and your own reputation.

There are three main groups of information you need to guard. On a macro level, there is overall information about how your organization operates: numbers, strategy, and plans. Within the organization, this information may be common currency, but it is good practice not to share it outside the walls unless it is ready to be public information, like in an annual report. Then there is specific information about current negotiations and deals. Often this should not be talked about beyond your immediate team, let alone outside the company. Finally, there are facts about individuals, such as salary and personal details, that should be shared with almost no one. Even in organizations where everything is available to everyone on the server, the personnel file is often the only one to be locked and password-protected.

Managing confidentiality is about guarding these kinds of information well until you are in a situation where it is appropriate to disclose them. There are no hard-and-fast rules, but in general the "need-to-know" principle works well: The time to let others know confidential information is when you need their support to work with you on something. It's tough to operate as a team unless everyone has shared knowledge of issues and events. This is trickier when you're working with an outside consultant or partner. They can be major leakers of information, through thoughtlessness rather than malicious behavior. Get them to sign confidentiality agreements, and give them guidelines to pass on to their staffs.

There is no such thing as a confidential conversation. Without becoming paranoid, you can take a few sensible precautions. Never discuss anything sensitive in a public place like an airplane or restaurant, since you never know who is nearby. And never talk to the press without preparation, in case you say something by accident. Nothing is truly "off the record" with most reporters.

The analogy of a dimmer switch can be useful when thinking about confidentiality. Many people seem to have on/off switches when it comes to spilling information: Once they've started saying something, they end up saying

There is no such thing as a confidential conversation.

it all and saying it again elsewhere. It's safer to imagine yourself gradually turning your dial up or down, releasing information at levels that you sense are appropriate. Trust your instincts. If you get a feeling that what you are saying or are about to say is at all controversial (for example, sometimes someone suddenly perks up and shows curiosity about something you thought he already knew), heed that feeling and turn down the switch, steering the conversation elsewhere.

PART IV

THE TRUTH ABOUT NETWORKING

TRUTH 17

GOOD NETWORKING IS ABOUT ENJOYING
THE CONVERSATION

In some cultures, networking is a way of life. In Asia, for example, business cards come out as soon as you meet someone. You establish who and what you both are and if you have any connections. That your network of relationships makes your reputation is openly acknowledged. In Western cultures, people are more cautious, wary of pushing themselves on others, or worried that their "networking" will come across as obvious. This can make them appear hesitant and tense unless they are with people they know.

Napier Collyns, cofounder of the networking organization Global Business Network, is an expert on forging connections. He maintains that the best mind-set for networking is "to be interested in people and their ideas" and then to "self-effacedly connect them with others whom you know." For Collyns, networking becomes mechanical if it's just about self-interest. The trick is to focus on other people's needs, pushing your own objectives to the back of your mind. You will have a chance to raise these once a relationship is formed. Concentrate on getting to know the other person, enjoying his company, and finding out what you can offer him.

Networking becomes mechanical if it's just about self-interest. The trick is to focus on other people's needs.

Collyns distinguishes between passive and active networking. Passive networking happens every time you talk with someone. Active networking is about talking with a specific purpose in mind. The more time you invest in the former, getting to know people during everyday events, the more robust your network gets, and the easier it is to start active networking. All the conversation positions you to connect people who can mutually benefit each other—and you too, of course!

Really great networkers network all the time. They love talking to people and finding out their stories. That's the key to passive networking. Unearthing someone's background and interests allows you to identify commonalities and to start building a history of shared conversations. If you're not gregarious by nature, you'll still find that if you take a deep breath, dive in, and ask friendly questions, nine times out of ten you'll get a good conversation going. Most people enjoy talking about themselves and welcome the opportunity to do so.

Once you know something beyond general niceties, it's much easier to remember someone. Good active networkers keep a mental catalog of people they've met, remembering who is interested in what, who would like to connect with whom, or who just likes having an interesting conversation. A business card reference system can help. As soon as you return from an event, go through any cards you acquired, seeing what you remember about each person. Write handy information on the backs of the cards while the encounter is still fresh in your mind. That way, the next time you meet someone who is looking for, say, a consultant to help with a venture in the Middle East, you may well know who to send her to! Don't forget to have cards of your own handy too.

It's easy to spot networkers who are motivated by pure self-interest. They often strike you as phony, even manipulative. They're the folks who look past you into the room as they shake your hand. Make sure that others don't gain that impression of you by being fully present in every conversation and by showing others the interest they deserve.

TRUTH 18

PEOPLE LOVE TO BE ASKED
THEIR OPINION

Take any topic, and almost anyone you ask will have an opinion. It's just human nature: Being opinionated helps each of us define our identity, and it's what differentiates us from, or connects us to, others. Fortunately, there are daily opportunities to offer opinions, from writing to the paper to keeping a blog (web log) to sitting at the bar debating topics with friends. We also contribute our opinions in the public realm by way of opinion polls, surveys, and elections.

Canvassing for opinions is one of the best ways to connect with others at work. People love being asked what they think, because it makes them feel important and valued, and they get to talk about themselves while someone listens with interest. They also enjoy it because it's so easy: there's no need to study or prepare much to have an opinion, and no there's need to back it up, either, since an opinion is just a point of view, not a test of knowledge.

Canvassing for opinions is one of the best ways to connect with others at work.

When you want to make something happen at work, asking for opinions is a way to generate the support and buy-in of others. Even better, asking for opinions from opinion makers—senior executives and heads of relevant departments—can help your ideas gain ground in the organization. If you talk to enough key people, you'll get a good sense of general feelings about the issue while also being able to help those folks understand your proposition or intent. Armed with their feedback, you are in a position to produce a discussion document, feeding information about your ideas back to both the opinion givers and the wider organization, generating more discussion. That document will be taken much more seriously if it contains opinions besides your own.

This opinion-gathering process works well even if you don't have a specific project to promote. It can help you position yourself as someone who asks good questions and cares about the company's future.

When gathering opinions, the key is to ask open-ended questions. These give the people you're asking lots of opportunity to talk, resulting in a good body of information. An open-ended question such as "How are things working since we restructured the IT system?" may give you a general or fuzzy answer initially. You can then probe for examples, actions taken as a result, and positive and negative impacts. You can also probe nonverbal clues like hesitation or shrugging. It's fine to say, "You seem a little hesitant; can you tell me more about that?"

You'll create more relationships in two months by being interested in people's opinions than you will in two years by trying to make them interested in you and what you do. Not only will the information gathered from those opinions be useful to you in many ways, but any actions you take as a result will show that you truly respect what those people have to say. Asking for opinions is win-win all the way around.

TRUTH 19

YOU HAVE CONNECTIONS TO MORE PEOPLE THAN YOU THINK

Stanley Milgram, a researcher at Yale University, conducted several unusual experiments in the 1960s. One project involved selecting an obscure name in a distant U.S. state and then asking nearly 300 students to work at finding this person's contact information. He found that the greatest number of people his students had to contact to reach anyone, anywhere in the country, was six. Although Dr. Milgram's theory has yet to be scientifically proven, its message has made headway into popular culture. It is now often said that there are only "six degrees of separation" between each of us and almost anyone in the world. What a fabulous resource we have!

So how can you use that resource in the workplace? It's no exaggeration to say that through all your potential connections you can learn

It is said that there are only "six degrees of separation" between each of us and almost anyone in the world.

about or accomplish almost anything. Someone out there will know what you need to know or can help you with what you need to do. If you want to find the best person for a project, or get support for a workplace initiative (to name just two possibilities), and you don't already know someone who can help you, the first thing to do is to start putting out feelers.

One high-level executive wanted to meet some influential people in government in Washington, D.C. to get support for legislation his company sorely needed. So the executive mapped all the people he knew in his company and then asked these associates to make a map of their direct and indirect connections with people in the government. Next, he asked for introductions to some of these connections so that he could consult with them directly. He quickly found the right people to network with to obtain the required introductions.

The place to start is with your existing network. It consists of all the professional colleagues you feel able to approach with a question or issue. It may be a small group of like-minded people you have known over the years, ranging from college classmates and professors to former colleagues. You can rely on people with whom you have a good relationship to introduce you to others whom they trust and respect.

Once you have the contact, accessing information and advice, or exerting influence, is easier than ever with the Internet. Its speed and ease of forwarding make it an ideal way to reach people anywhere in the world. Be aware, however, that when someone is far away from you, personally or geographically, you may need to put a "frame," or explanation, around your request to help others understand your thinking.

You may also need to be more formal in tone. Be sure to check on the communication and networking protocols of other countries.

One savvy American executive wanted to hire a general manager to run his company's Chinese business. His first step was to ask everyone he knew in Beijing, Shanghai, and Hong Kong to suggest candidates. He then checked their suggestions with headhunters. Having tracked down the ideal person, the American then used his newly extended Chinese network to work on convincing the desired executive that the position was right for him. Impressed by the offer and the American's *guanxi*, or connections, the Chinese executive took the job.

There are many examples of how using the six degrees of separation rule can help you make things happen. Connections are endlessly useful at work and are essential in some cultures. Using them is not just about accessing facts, knowledge, or staff. People with different backgrounds or experiences can also help you think through your work or ideas by offering you alternative perspectives. Such touchstones are invaluable.

TRUTH 20

COMMONALITIES
CEMENT RELATIONSHIPS

We have something in common with most everyone we meet, from secretaries to presidents of companies. Unearthing those commonalities is a very effective way of building good relationships with people at work. That goes for people you've known for a while, people you've just met, and even people you haven't met yet but would like to get to know.

Commonalities are points of connection that broaden relationships beyond the basic information exchanges of working life. While those exchanges tend to take place on an impersonal cerebral level, finding ways to touch people where their values and experiences matter to them helps you develop a stronger personal bond. We each have parts of our background and interests we can highlight in order to connect with others, from where we grew up, or have worked and traveled, to what we've read or studied, or even to the teams we root for.

Frieda, a young manager working overseas, was frustrated by how "hard it is to get noticed in a crowded multinational company when you're outside the head office." Having observed how mentors had helped other young executives in her company, she decided that she needed similar support. But what was she to do when she had never worked at headquarters or met any of the top guys? However, she *had* gone to Stanford University for an executive MBA, so she decided to use her Ivy League experience as her ticket to find a mentor. She would connect with others in her company who shared that background.

Using the alumni rosters, Frieda set up appointments for career discussions with every executive on those lists. After one round of meetings, at which she asked for support in getting known at the head office, she found herself a mentor. As a result of his opening doors, Frieda enjoyed career discussions with people at the top of the company. After a year and a half, she was promoted to a country manager role and is perfectly positioned for the job she wants next. Frieda admits that making this happen was tough. But once she asked for support, life got easier.

Connections can be established both directly and indirectly. A direct approach is to ask people questions, particularly at social events. Every function is an opportunity to make connections, and unlike the workplace, these are environments where all you are expected to do is talk. Once you are in a position to chat with someone, politely find out enough about her background and interests to be able to respond to her in ways that show you have similar experiences, views, or qualifications. And don't forget

Every social function is an opportunity to make connections.

to get back to the people you meet. It pays to always carry business cards and to ask for them when you meet people.

Indirect approaches involve researching and observing. Use your networks to ask about key people, or "Google" them before business meetings or parties. You'll be surprised by the wealth of information available, both personal and professional. Careful daily observation also gives you great information about people you don't yet know well. What pictures do they have in their offices? What books are they reading? What photos do they have on their desks?

There is always a way to find a commonality. People have even been known to connect through infirmities. For example, when neither you nor your dining companion at a corporate dinner can eat the peanut sauce or drink the red wine, you can always connect over your strong reactions to these things!

TRUTH 21

SOCIAL TALK IS
SOCIAL GREASE

Social talk is a general term for small talk, or light conversation. In an office situation, it's any kind of talk that is not task-oriented, from pleasantries exchanged on arrival in the morning, to chatting around the coffeemaker, to snippets of conversation with clients before getting down to business at a meeting. However, don't let the words "light" or "small" deceive you; your ability to engage in social talk can have a *big* impact on your work relationships.

Social talk can come to the rescue when you don't know exactly what to say to strangers and acquaintances but you want to start a conversation or keep one going. It allows you to connect with others and make them feel at ease. Never believe that when your mind is on business that social talk is a waste of time. At the beginning of a business meeting, chatting about the weather or a current event can

Your ability to engage in social talk can have a big impact on your work relationships.

ease you into the conversation, improving the quality of the serious discussion that follows.

There will be moments when social talk is the main purpose of a work occasion, such as an evening reception or a sports event. Partners or clients may often be present. When that is the case, it can be tempting, and appear natural, to talk about business issues. Americans tend to jump into work and money discussions easily. However, in many other cultures it is socially unacceptable to talk openly about money, sex, politics, or other sensitive issues. If you do so with British clients, for example, you may just succeed in making them uncomfortable.

If you have major client relationships in particular countries, it's worth talking with people from the region, including secretaries, to determine how much time is spent in social talk and what topics are acceptable. In Latin America, for instance, social talk about personal lives is the normal way to start the day. You'll find that one half-hour of checking in with people to find out how they and their families are doing will make it easier to get work done for the rest of the day.

Even without advance planning, a skilled social talker can stay on firm ground with people of all cultures, including Americans, by having a repertoire of neutral social talk at the ready. Questions about children and national customs are both good topics. Two other "safe" themes that you can prepare in advance are current events and personal interests. Be ready with questions and thoughts about both.

Confidence in current affairs comes from reading everything you can find, from newspapers and biographies to catalogs and cookbooks. Focus on what interests you so that you can talk enthusiastically about it. Just reading reviews of TV programs and books is a great way to develop opinions about topical issues. This positions you to say "I just heard the most interesting statistic" or "I just read the most fascinating thing," which usually leads to a discussion.

Confident personal talk comes from having a list of questions ready to ask about someone's occupation, family, or pastimes. Make sure to remember the answers; people will be touched if you refer to these again in the future. Be prepared to talk about yourself too, with answers ready for questions posed to you. If this kind of talk doesn't come naturally, memorize answers in advance, practicing on family and friends to ensure that they come out smoothly. Prepare a 30- to 60-second "elevator pitch"—a little speech the length of an average elevator ride—that you can roll out about yourself.

There are also many low-risk situations where you can practice outside the company of acquaintances. The more intimate the situation, the easier it will be, since closeness makes people talk more readily. Talk with strangers in your doctor's waiting room, when standing in line, or when at the airport. Asking people about the book or article they're reading is always a good opener.

Social talk is worth preparing and practicing. The more you hone and try out what you will say, the more trippingly it will roll off your tongue, and the more natural it will sound.

PART V

THE TRUTH
ABOUT GETTING
THINGS DONE

TRUTH 22

"Closing the Sale" Is About Gauging the Right Moment to Ask for What You Want

A highly successful communications chief at a large U.S. government agency started his career selling Fuller Brushes door-to-door. Rather than hide his humble past, he attributes his career success to those first hard lessons learned from selling. The experience of "cold calling"—the daily routine of knocking on a door, trying to sell something, and coping with rejection—helped him hone skills that proved invaluable to him in all future jobs, sales-related or not.

Whatever your job, much of your time at work is dedicated to "selling" things to others, whether those things are ideas, projects, or even yourself. Salespeople often say that closing the sale is the toughest part of their role. That goes for all those work negotiations too. How do you efficiently and effectively get to a point where hands are shaken, your idea is chosen, a new initiative is agreed on, or you're offered a raise? The truth is that there is no easy formula. However, two pieces of advice hold true. First, you must openly and explicitly ask for what you want. If you don't ask, you won't get. The second is that you need to ask when the time is right.

Asking for the sale is about focus. On the one hand, this means being absolutely sure of what you want to make happen and holding this goal in your head the whole time you are speaking. On the other hand, it means noticing how the other person is responding to you and your words as you develop a sense of rapport that takes you both toward the sale.

The trick is to gradually move that other person toward commitment, closing the sale stage by stage. The more difficult the sell, the more stages you need. Rather than try to get to the endgame upfront, convey elements of your idea one by one, finding agreement on each, at a rate that is comfortable to the "customer." Every time he or she nods his or her head, smiles, or shows interest in even a small part of your story, you gain a positive "vote" and are one step closer to commitment to the broader theme. When you feel you have gathered a good number of votes and that the customer understands and trusts you, it's time to push for the real "sale."

> *The trick is to gradually move the other person toward commitment, closing the sale stage by stage.*

Catharine managed a mortgage services department. With a batch of mortgages "at risk," she wanted to sell the idea of having an additional person in her group do an ongoing risk review. However, her company saw all risk as a central, shared function. Catharine made her case over two months by gradually letting her boss know the potential financial exposure if something went wrong. Her boss became curious about the numbers involved and felt comfortable with Catharine's analysis. When she finally asked for the additional staff, he said, "I was waiting for you to ask."

Curious and comfortable are the key words from this story, and you should consider them when closing the sale. You achieve curiosity and comfort by researching people before you approach them to determine their key concerns. You can then refer to these in your interaction. This tactic reassures them that you understand them and the company and helps you clearly present them with a rationale to pique their interest. This makes them want to continue talking with you because they sense that it may be in their, and the company's, best interest.

Many of us flinch at the idea of "selling" because we don't like pushing people. That instinct is correct. Forceful tactics provoke resistance from others, making them reluctant to continue talking. The smart seller carefully builds a rapport with the other party over time, gradually gaining his or her trust and support. Then, when the moment is right, the most natural and sensible thing in the world is to ask.

TRUTH 23

PUTTING THE BOTTOM LINE FIRST LEADS TO FOCUSED ACTION

The "bottom line" is the last line of a financial statement. It shows the net profit or loss of a company or organization. In most businesses the state of that bottom line is a fundamental reference point, an indicator of success or failure. Nonprofit organizations and charities know that the buck stops here because if they drift into the red they won't have the resources to deliver their objectives.

In daily transactions at work, financial objectives are not always the main focus. Immediate goals may involve completing a report, launching a project, or selling an idea. Nevertheless, every activity has a "bottom line," or endgame, of its own, albeit metaphorically, and it's important to understand what this is. A report for clients on a new initiative, for example, has a very different endgame than a report for internal consumption. They both aim to report, but the former's bottom line is probably "selling," and the latter's may be "learning." You need to be clear which one you are trying to achieve. Establishing the endgame focuses attention and effort on what really counts, helping you, and others, achieve what you need in as efficient a way as possible.

When working with others, putting the bottom line first is an invaluable strategy. Clearly communicating the endgame sets a deliberate and logical approach, focusing colleagues' minds as well as your own. People know what they need to achieve and why. This empowers them to act. For example, if ease of application for busy executives is the bottom line for an internal human resources evaluation initiative, you should emphasize that point in any briefing, ensuring that whatever your colleagues do, they consider how they are meeting that goal. You would alert them to the need to avoid procedures that have complex guidelines or lots of forms to fill out. However useful such details might be in terms of the evaluation, the tactics would ultimately work against your endgame.

Clearly communicating the endgame sets a deliberate and logical approach, focusing colleagues' minds as well as your own.

The more focused on the bottom line your briefing is, the more quickly and efficiently you can encourage others to get there. When a project is important, it is often tempting to give others a lot of information about the task, concluding the briefing with what you want to have happen. The result is that all the "getting it done" energy loses steam. If you need people to take ownership of a task quickly, giving them the bottom line first creates a mental hook on which they can hang the facts and details that follow. For example, when asking Finance to come up with a new IT program to track budget expenditures for your non-numerically minded team, you might start your briefing by stressing that you need an easy-to-use tool to monitor spending that individuals can use without supervision. With that shared picture, you can then explore together how it might work.

Stating the bottom line first lays out an argument in a way that makes sense and compels you or another party to take action. It's worth taking the time—however busy you are, however multifaceted the project, or however close the deadline—to figure out exactly what you are trying to achieve, rather than just diving straight in with facts and data. Focus energy up front on the bottom line, and you'll get focused action in return.

TRUTH 24

OBSTACLES AT WORK ARE THERE TO BE NEGOTIATED

When Bugs Bunny runs into a wall or gets hit by a steamroller, does he lie down quietly? No. He picks himself up, pulls himself back into shape, and thinks of a new way to get the carrots! For Bugs and many other popular cartoon characters, no setback is too difficult. That mind-set makes them great role models for coping with obstacles at work. A successful executive has the stamina and initiative to keep looking for another way through.

Being stonewalled at work is all too common. You're stonewalled when someone says he won't pay for something, that you can't do something, or that's not how things are done. This may seem like a dead end, but never become discouraged. Giving up is a sure way to lose career focus. If the project is important, you can take action to help secure support for it, or even find a compromise that benefits you in other ways.

How you tackle a stonewaller has a lot to do with how important his or her support is to your plans. If the person is your boss, and you want to make departmental changes or need money, it is vital to bring him or her onboard by one means or another.

How you tackle a stonewaller has a lot to do with how important his or her support is to your plans.

Recognize this scenario? You're in the middle of implementing an agreed-upon strategy, when, at a crucial moment, your boss suddenly tells you to cut costs or head count before year's end. Knocks the wind out of your sails, doesn't it? The next time something similar happens, before doing or saying anything, ask yourself the following questions: If I stop now, will my work be irreparably undone? Is the project vital to my group's success? Will the changes negatively affect other parts of the company? If you answer yes to any of these, it is in your best interests to push back.

When pushing back, understanding the reasons for the stonewall helps you position yourself. For example, if your boss is the type to deliberately set obstacles to encourage employees to fight for their beliefs, tell him what you think with clear objectives and total calm. If he thinks it is his job to save money for the firm, and he is focused on cutting costs, he may be harder to sway. In that case, conceding cuts on one project may help you secure support for other initiatives, keeping them on track. If your boss is a bully who says no just because he can, your best bet is to present your case to him firmly, confidently, and without emotion. If you make it clear that you can't be pushed around, he may decide it's not worth the effort.

When straight talk doesn't work, think laterally. An effective—albeit time-consuming—tactic is to line up support from influential colleagues of your boss whose own projects may be affected by the change. Approach them for advice, discuss the pros and cons, and then secure their support *in writing* before presenting a reinforced case to your boss. It's much harder to stonewall efforts that are supported by influential others. More often than not, your boss will back down.

When the obstacle in your path is a peer or subordinate, your options increase. If his or her cooperation is not crucial, you may be able to drop the relationship, avoiding further conflict. If you decide to argue the case, stay above the fray by citing company principles that work in your favor rather than getting personal, or find influential people who can support you. To keep the situation from recurring, consider setting some mutual ground rules to help you deal with future disagreements.

Staying in the game no matter what the obstacles or detours is a career builder. Finding ways around obstacles is even better and helps you hone your strategic abilities.

TRUTH 25

SUPPORT STAFF DESERVE GIVE AS WELL AS TAKE

Ever seen the workplace movie *Nine to Five?* Or maybe you've heard its catchy theme song, sung by Dolly Parton, lamenting the fact that for assistants at work it's often "all taking and no giving." Humorous as it is, there's truth in that song. If you want to get the most out of support staff, you need to ensure that your relationship with them is not a selfish one. Your treatment of administrators, clerks, and assistants can prove a real career builder or buster.

Support staff are vital members of your team, whether they work directly for you or in the IT department or mail room. They are the ones who keep you on your game, remembering key dates, people, and other information. They are also there on the front lines, meeting the public and dealing with clients. Support staff with a long tenure are often an impressive source of knowledge about company and department history and detail. Last but not least, support staff talk with lots of other people in your organization! This all means that, from a career point of view, an annoyed administrator can make your life very difficult. It also means that once you find support staff who prioritize and follow through well, you have found gold. So treat them as such.

How do you show appreciation to support staff? At the simplest level, you display common courtesy by greeting them and recognizing special occasions like birthdays. Notice them, pass the time of day, and treat them with the respect you would show any professional. Small things make a difference. You should develop this rapport with all staff, not only those you are directly in charge of. Make an effort to empathize with them, to think about how you would want to be treated or spoken to if you were in their position. Then act accordingly.

When it comes to doing the work, clear instructions with specific deadlines and quality parameters make life much easier for support staff. If you want an administrator to send a memo to everyone at the meeting, tell him or her—don't just assume. Discuss the recurring items on your schedule rather than expecting to be told every time. And give him or her enough time to get things done, keeping high urgency to rare occasions. If you e-mail a request for something the night before you need it, you cannot fairly expect it to be done first thing the next day. (Sadly, such requests are not uncommon!)

> *How do you show appreciation to support staff? Small things make a difference.*

A major sign of respect is to offer an avenue for development. One of the most interesting training deals I've come across was something called the "Support Staff Institute." This monthly lunchtime training, brown bag lunch included, started with computer updates and moved to briefing about the activities of each department, with a final session where the president came to talk about the company's future. Support staff managed and ran the program with advice from training and development. It was cheap and easy and had high payoff for very little time investment.

Finally, what are the big no-no's in working with support staff? Above all, don't expect support staff to read your mind (although, amazingly, some seem to with time). Blaming and shaming can also generate frustration and distrust. Never blame your staff when something doesn't work out or try to shame them for making a mistake. If you examine your motives, your urge to do this probably comes from your frustration with yourself. Venting this may make you feel better temporarily but will not serve your reputation or your relationships in the long term. As for when things go right, make sure that you acknowledge the role of staff in that success. Returning to *Nine to Five*, make sure that you're not the "boss who takes the credit." That really drives support staff crazy!

PART VI

THE TRUTH ABOUT MANAGING YOUR WORKLOAD

TRUTH 26

GOOD PRIORITIZING MEANS FACTORING URGENCY AGAINST IMPORTANCE

Do you find yourself having to rush around to fix problem after problem? Are you always fighting fires, so that you never have time to focus on the really big issues on your list? The obvious answer, and it's nothing revolutionary, is to prioritize your workload: Make clear choices about what to do in what order. However, effective prioritizing is easier said than done.

Good prioritizing requires an understanding of the interplay between urgency and importance. At first glance, many of the tasks you face each day may seem equally urgent and important. Yet, on closer inspection, you'll realize that some urgent ones are really not that important. Likewise, the things that are most important in the long run are often not that urgent. However busy your working day is, it's a time-saver in the long run to regularly stop and consider this interplay in order to focus on the things that really count.

Urgent tasks are those with immediate deadlines, such as renewing a membership before it expires. Important tasks are those that may not have a pressing deadline but that will help you achieve long-term goals, or that have implications for your career, such as networking with key people. A few tasks are both urgent and important, such as finishing your performance review because it is due tomorrow. However, whether or not they are important, we tend to deal with urgent tasks first, because their urgency jumps out at us.

Good prioritizing is not about ignoring urgency. It's about working out which (very few) tasks are both important and urgent—those that will get you into a fix if you don't do them—and tackling them first. After tackling these tasks, you should focus some time on the important but nonurgent tasks—the ones that can be rewarding in the long run—while keeping one eye on any other urgent tasks to ensure that no deadlines are missed. Ideally, you might delegate some of those to others.

Urgent tasks have immediate deadlines. Important tasks may not have a pressing deadline but will help you achieve long-term goals.

Drawing a chart like the one shown here will help you categorize tasks. Place each task that you need to accomplish on the chart axes, weighing importance versus urgency as you go. The closer to the upper-right corner a task is, the sooner you start it. You should aim to achieve something in that high-importance/high-urgency box and to make some progress in the high-importance/low-urgency box every day. No matter how much fun it would be to forward that funny e-mail, don't be distracted by low-urgency, low-importance tasks until you have cleared the other boxes.

One further aid to effective prioritizing is the Pareto Principle, or the "80/20 rule." This says that 80% of measurable results come from just 20% of your activity. Likewise, 80% of your business comes from 20% of your clients. So it's worth taking time to identify the few important tasks—that 20%—that will lead to the greatest payoff. Focus on these and do them as soon as you can. These tasks will get you noticed in the organization and thus have the greatest impact on your career.

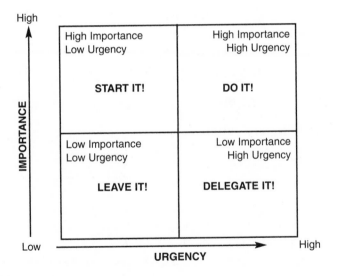

TRUTH 27

KNOWING HOW TO SAY NO IS A KEY TIME-MANAGEMENT TOOL

N o. It's just one little word. So why do we find it so hard to say, particularly when we're at work?

Why do we find it so hard to say no, particularly when we're at work?

Well, to start, it's tough to be the bearer of bad news. Negative words are more powerful than positive ones. Their impact is like a cold shower: People may tense up, stop listening, or get defensive. You don't want to be the bad guy of the office by dismissing your colleagues' proposals. Nor do you want to upset senior executives who might influence your career progress.

However, not knowing how to say no can be a recipe for workplace stress and career chaos. If you say yes to everything, you may never have time to properly do the things that really matter, or to think strategically about your future actions. On the other hand, being known as someone who sets (and who helps others set) clear priorities and boundaries will earn you respect and help your career.

The key is knowing when and how to say no. Doing it well is about clarity, courtesy, and careful choices. Be seen as being fair by having consistent standards, whether those are industry practices, ethical considerations, or just the way you always do things. That way, you won't have to argue the facts every time. But do consider each request thoughtfully, weighing possible consequences in terms of both the business and your own role. Your decision may depend on who's asking and how much of an opportunity you may be passing up. Then, after you've made an informed decision, stick to it. Change your mind only if something very high-priority shows up.

Careful consideration may even help you find a compromise. Time, cost, quantity, and quality can be flexible project parameters. Is the case as urgent or necessary as it was first presented? Push back on expectations. If they want it in one day, suggest two. You get "wiggle room" by pushing boundaries, and you gain respect when you can't be taken advantage of. When you'd like to be responsive but lack resources, offer alternatives. Can you meet part of but not the entire request? Can someone else help?

It's not uncommon for finance directors to be faced with dilemmas when their departments are asked to take on one more project. There may be a time when a finance department is overloaded while they are installing a new

You get "wiggle room" by pushing boundaries, and you gain respect when you can't be taken advantage of.

computer system and while running their day-to-day operations. They may be faced with the pressure of fulfilling their commitments while being consistent and fair in supporting other departments. Finance might start with an offer to do the project later and then, if needed, offer to go the extra mile to pay for a consultant charge to ensure that the project gets done in time.

Other advice? Think twice before doing favors. It can backfire: You're likely to be asked for more and more and be seen as a pushover. Sadly, the more helpful you are, the less others value what you give. And look out for "orphans"—projects that are floundering and need to be taken in hand. There's usually a reason that they have no home, and it's not your job to give them one. They will bring no glory!

It's easy to get upset if you are annoyed by a request, or feel guilty for turning it down, but don't let saying no become an emotional issue. Knowing how to say no calmly and diplomatically is a professional skill that brings both practical benefits in the short term and career respect and responsibility over time.

TRUTH 28

GOOD FENCES MAKE GOOD NEIGHBORS: BE CLEAR ON ROLES AND RESPONSIBILITIES

The poet Robert Frost used the old New England expression "Good fences make good neighbors" in a poem about mending fences. Good fences clearly define property boundaries, reducing trespass and conflicts over ownership. Clear boundaries are just as important for your career, especially when working alongside others. With the exception of some unionized, government, and low-level jobs, few sets of workplace roles and responsibilities are perfectly defined. And the smaller the organization, the fuzzier the lines can get.

However, that's not always a bad thing. A good workplace fence is solid but flexible, such as not making coffee for your boss each morning but helping out when there are visitors. Boundaries can be moved to serve you and the organization, as long as everyone knows that the lines are shifting and why. That way, no one's toes get stepped on, and no one gets overloaded. Flexible fences ensure that key tasks don't get neglected in the white space between jobs on the organization chart. They also offer you opportunities to contribute in areas of expertise beyond those of your main job, assisting your career development. If you're great with customers, for example, and you want to get into management, you need to show ability in other areas, such as budgeting. It's your responsibility to look out for chances to hone and showcase your talents, but also to ensure that you don't end up doing someone else's job on top of your own in the process.

Taking on too much job overlap is common among overachievers and naïve newcomers. In the first case it won't win you friends, and in the second it sets a dangerous precedent. Susan was a new human resources manager who spent three days creating a spreadsheet that mapped the cost of employee head-count changes. Her bosses were delighted and asked that she update the spreadsheet weekly. This seemed reasonable enough to them, since Susan was aware of everyone who was coming and going. However, Susan, wary of a time-consuming extension to her job boundaries, wisely proposed a compromise. She would supply the names of people on the move each week, but someone from Finance could slice and dice the numbers on a spreadsheet.

Good boundary-setting is about defining your areas of expertise and delegating the rest. But that can be tough

Good boundary-setting is about defining your areas of expertise and delegating the rest.

to achieve, especially early in your career. When fuzzy boundaries start causing problems, particularly with clients, you may need to bring in your boss, human resources, or an outside facilitator to flush out misunderstandings, gaps, and overlaps, and objectively chart roles and responsibilities. Such a process helps reduce conflict by creating an external focus for discussion, rather than pitting individuals against each other.

A formal charting process of the players works when you really need it. The rest of the time, you and your boss need to agree on your job parameters. Then it's your responsibility to keep your fences in good repair by consistently defining your job against that of others, showcasing your strengths whenever boundaries can be pushed, but not letting others push you around.

TRUTH 29

GOOD FILING SAVES YOUR TIME AND YOUR REPUTATION

Ever spent time looking for an important folder at work? Or searched frantically through piles of paper for something you know was there yesterday? People may think of filing as a small thing: a tedious administrative task that is not the best use of professional time. On the contrary, filing is the glue that connects past to present in organizational life.

Filing is the glue that connects past to present in organizational life.

Filing is a vehicle that allows you to find information when you need it. Good filing means creating a framework that will allow your future self to quickly and efficiently retrieve what you need. So before you or your assistant set up a system, stop and ask yourself how you, and others, will need to use the information in the future. The word "others" is key, since fellow team members need to understand the files, as will anyone to whom you later hand over a project. The absent-minded professor who has papers piled to the ceiling but can still locate anything is a romantic ideal—fine if you are the only one needing information, but problematic as soon as others are involved. Those piles on your desk can also label you as a "messy thinker."

There is no perfect filing system, so don't get hung up on creating one. But good labeling is fundamental, whether files are on your computer, on your desk, or in a cabinet. Name each folder or subfolder as soon as you create it. If you can't think what to call something, take 5 seconds to let the first word you associate with the matter pop into your mind. This instinctive label will probably be what occurs to you when you look for that information again. If someone else does your filing, make sure that the two of you agree on labels and locations, because that person might not think like you do. Finally, when there's a connection between electronic and paper files, be sure to use the same name. This may sound obvious, but it's amazing how many people don't do it.

The pre-computer age had fewer filing options. Finding things was often more straightforward, but also more time-consuming. The information age has brought many different options and tools, from e-mail storage systems to zip discs, from shared systems on servers to intricate databases. Once you understand and agree on the use of these electronic aids, you can have all kinds of information at your fingertips.

Regularly use the layered folders available on your computer to classify information, rather than just dumping everything in My Documents or on your desktop. On a more strategic level, seek the advice of IT staff on how to create an efficient strategy for storing information. This is particularly vital for archiving—filing for things you no longer need every day, but may need to get your hands on quickly. For example, technology may allow you to archive old documents in a way that doesn't take up space in current folders but that still can be easily accessed via your computer.

Whatever you do with long-term filing has got to be better than the old days, when paper files were put in storage. Not only were the files hard to find, but they often came to you after quite a delay, covered in dust and mold.

TRUTH 30

PROMISES MADE, PROMISES KEPT: FINISHING ON TIME MATTERS

Ever worked late into the night on an assignment, sweating to finish something as the hours tick by? Almost everyone has pushed to meet a deadline. We push ourselves because we know deadlines matter. But beyond that short-term panic, how many of us stop and consider quite how much they matter?

True professionals understand that finishing on time is a fundamental promise of business. Barring fire, flood, or earthquake, if you make a commitment to do something at work, you should do everything you can to get it done, and done on time. Failure to do so not only causes short-term problems for the organization and embarrassment for you, but in the long term, repeatedly missed deadlines can damage

True professionals understand that finishing on time is a fundamental promise of business.

your reputation. Colleagues and bosses may decide that they cannot trust you enough to involve you in the future, meaning that you miss out on opportunities for advancement.

A professional attitude means playing safe by starting each task well in advance of its deadline, rather than waiting until the last minute. This is partly because, however efficient you may be, few assignments rely on your input alone. In most cases you will be working with others, and others can be unpredictable and hard to control, even when they report to you. Starting ahead of time allows you to accommodate or remedy their mistakes and delays.

Pressure of work, or the need to access specific skills, may sometimes mean that you hand over a whole task to someone else. When delegating or reassigning, it's up to you to take responsibility for this subcontractor relationship and ensure that the new person completes the task. It may be off your To Do list, but red-flag it for follow-up on your calendar so that you remember to check on its progress.

Despite good intentions, in reality it can often be hard to initiate a project early on, particularly when your schedule is packed. The new project can seem just too big to tackle until you can clear a good stretch of time. When that is the case, you need to divide and conquer. A proven way to make a major task less daunting is to divide it into a number of bite-size parts to be dealt with one at a time. If you have a report to write, for instance, brainstorm all your thoughts and ideas first. Then identify the major themes and sections and plan a separate writing session for each, as if they were unique pieces of writing. As soon as you have the first thing down on paper, the report will feel as if it's moving forward, and the challenge will feel smaller.

From time to time, something unexpected will happen, and, despite your best efforts, you cannot meet a commitment. People can accept this as long as you give them forewarning and suggest a new date that is acceptable to everyone. A general guideline is to alert people before you reach the halfway mark. On a six-week project, for example, you should let people know if you might be late no later than three weeks in. So keep your professional radar on, and sense what is coming up on the work horizon.

Your personal integrity is on the line with every promise or agreement you make. If you get a reputation for being undependable, it's hard to shake.

PART VII

THE TRUTH ABOUT GETTING YOUR POINT ACROSS

TRUTH 31

THE MEDIUM REALLY IS THE MESSAGE: MATCH YOUR MESSAGE TO YOUR AUDIENCE

Culture and communication guru Marshall McLuhan famously said, "The medium is the message," stressing that it's not *what* you say that counts, but *how* you say it. In business this is as true as anywhere else. From your tone of voice to the paper you write it on, the way in which you send a message to someone does a great deal to influence its effectiveness. That's because brains understand messages better when they are in the right medium for them.

Research has shown that we use our brains differently for different kinds of input. Most people have a preferred way of taking in information: by seeing it—in which case they are "visual" first, by hearing it—"auditory" first, or by "getting a feel" for it—kinesthetic first, meaning that they need to use their body in some way to fully engage. When receiving information in our preferred way, our brains are in a focused state called "beta." When we are less focused, our brains are more open to new ideas, in a state called "alpha." When we are addressed via our least-preferred media input, our brains enter a meditative state called "theta."

Most of us would prefer any audience at work to be as focused as possible. So how do we ensure that this is the case? By matching the medium to the audience.

For example, for those whose beta mode is to see or read information, a long meeting with lots of talking can make the mind drift. If their theta (least-focused) mode is listening, it's even harder to stay focused. That's when slides or other visual aids work well: You can focus people with charts, graphs, and bullet points. However, if someone's theta mode is visual, he or she may get impatient after more than a few slides, or turned off by long written reports, and may prefer to talk things over to digest information.

> *A long meeting with lots of talking can make the mind drift.*

You determine what medium people prefer by observing them while they are in meetings with you or in conversation with others. Anyone with a habit of doodling, pen-tapping, foot-jiggling, or getting up and walking around is likely to need to get a feel for things. All that movement keeps their brains in beta mode. People who cock their heads to one side may prefer to listen. At a more subtle level, eye movements are also helpful. Auditory people tend to look to one side while taking in information, while people who are visual often stare off into space. Colleagues who like to get a feel for things may look downward toward their dominant hand.

When addressing groups, things get more complicated. How do you engage everyone at the same time? The answer is to design some elements of your presentation to engage each type. A concise talk and accompanying slide show, with a time for group discussion, a few minutes for people to stretch their legs, or even workshop-style activities, offers the necessary variety. Or, more strategically, target the medium used toward the preferred communication method of key audience members.

What goes for others goes for you too. It's worth working out your own preferences, perhaps by asking someone to observe you. Aim to put yourself in beta mode when you need to concentrate, in alpha mode when you want to brainstorm and get creative, and in theta mode when you want to zone out and relax your brain.

TRUTH 32

PEOPLE REMEMBER BEGINNINGS AND ENDINGS

"I have a dream," said Martin Luther King, introducing his most famous speech. "Four score and seven years ago..." began the Gettysburg Address. Good speechwriters know that an engaging piece of text needs a "hook": something that pulls in the listener or reader right from the start, paving the way for what is to come. In those famous speeches of American history, those initial hooks successfully evoked a vision in others' minds of the nation's past and future.

An engaging piece of text needs a "hook": something that pulls in the listener or reader.

While the speeches you make at work may not be headed for the National Archives, nor address such significant audiences, every one of them requires your maximum attention to ensure that it puts your audience where you want them. Studies have shown that most people, whether reading or hearing text, tend to remember the words at the beginning and end more than the rest. This means that every time you pick up a pen or walk onto a podium, you need to use those crucial "start" and "finish" connection moments to your advantage so that others walk away with the messages you want to convey and remember you as a good communicator.

If anything, the words that come first grab the audience's attention. Use these to set the stage, just like those great speechwriters. Your hook doesn't have to be a grand statement; a joke, story, or interesting fact can work just as well, pulling the reader or listener in to the content that follows. Journalists tend to be masters of the effective hook, so a good way to get inspired is by studying magazine articles to see how the writers draw your attention.

A bit of personal disclosure can also draw people in. Rather than launch into facts and theory, you can begin with an anecdote or example pertinent to the points you are about to present. Telling your audience how your seven-year-old daughter asked you what would happen to her if you died, for example, might segue into all kinds of presentations about planning for the future, from career development to financial security. Even small bits of personal disclosure give your audience a connection to you and a human story to engage with. Once you think you have a good introduction, test it on trusted colleagues to see how the words play out.

The last few lines are your opportunity to sum up the key points of your message and fix those clearly in people's memories. There's no harm in being explicit. We've all heard speakers say, "And in conclusion, you need to remember three things..." or "If there's one thing I'd like you to take away, it's..." That's because these work: They focus people, through all the words and ideas, on the nub of the matter. For even more impact, you might connect those words with the actions you want others to take. You might suggest, "Here are the three steps that each of us needs to take in the next month." Send off the reader or listener inspired and ready to get to work.

Today's notoriously short attention spans have been shaped by television and the Internet. Don't fight this trend; keep your beginnings and endings snappy and memorable, with short sentences and catchy phrases. Think of them as the bookends of your text, providing a frame for all the fascinating information they support and enclose.

TRUTH 33

IT PAYS TO GET PEOPLE IN THE RIGHT FRAME OF MIND

An executive walks into a meeting and says, "The goal of this meeting is to finalize details and sign off on our plan. The meeting will have a 'hard finish' at two o'clock." Those two sentences quickly and efficiently focus the minds of all present, setting a frame for what needs to happen. The goals are tangible, and participants gain a shared sense of urgency and readiness. By the time the meeting ends, 5 minutes ahead of schedule, the plan is honed and ready to go.

"Framing" is the art of establishing clear direction or meaning. Whether you are giving a speech, making a request, or putting forward an argument, carefully chosen words can generate a context,

> *"Framing" is the art of establishing clear direction or meaning.*

or "frame," that highlights the central points of the matter at hand, just as a picture frame contains and highlights a picture. Skillful framing focuses the thinking of others, increasing the likelihood that they will achieve the goals, or give the response, you want from them. It is a knack well worth acquiring.

There are many forms of framing. The simplest one—a few words that "prime" what you are about to say—is useful when giving guidance, making simple requests, or asking questions, especially if the topic is remotely new or controversial. A good priming frame makes clear the purpose behind your request or comment. It also addresses the listener's concerns. So, when talking to a colleague, you might indicate that your request is a way to further a team goal. An example might be as follows: "It's going to be tough, but we need to complete this project by next week to fulfill our commitment to the Finance Department. I'm depending on your help to achieve this." Once someone buys into your frame, everything gets easier.

One effective way to help people buy into your message is to employ a story or metaphor as a frame that grabs the imagination. Many good communicators use metaphors that reflect interests or hobbies. Sports, sailing, and biblical analogies are all popular. A folksy leader may talk about the crops, seasons, or animals on a farm to illustrate a point.

A good story-frame strikes a balance between what works for you and situations with which your listener can identify. When Abraham Lincoln ran for president, he framed himself as someone who had pulled himself up by his bootstraps from humble origins in a log cabin. An incredibly articulate speaker, Lincoln had a knack for coming across as one of the people, despite his power and wealth. By introducing an element of self-disclosure to his public speeches—stressing his time in the "school of hard knocks"—Lincoln quickly generated trust and respect from his listeners, many of whom identified with his story.

Framing can also be a tactical way to respond to a provocative or difficult question from someone else, particularly if the way in which your response is interpreted may have negative repercussions for you or someone else. For instance, if someone asks you whether you think your boss has made a bad decision, there really is no right answer. Your response should be to frame the discussion by moving it into an objective or neutral gear. So you might respond, "Knowing that Jean always wants the best for the department, and given what she understood about that situation, I can understand why she might have made that decision." Taking a step back to frame helps defuse tension.

Successful frames can be as simple as a mention of the context or the reason for saying something or as complex as stories with metaphors. With practice, use of them becomes automatic, and you become a more successful and influential communicator.

TRUTH 34

SOME QUESTIONS ARE ACTUALLY STATEMENTS: BE READY FOR THEM

You've just given a great presentation at work. You feel good. Then, all of a sudden, although you've considered possible questions beforehand, a colleague asks you one that hits you right between the eyes. He asks if you have stopped having pollution problems. The tone is antagonistic rather than curious. As far as you know, there's never been any real problem with pollution. So what's that all about? And what do you do?

You might think that the primary aim of a question is to gain information. Wrong! In many public-speaking situations, the questions people ask actually function as statements: attempts to convey information rather than request it. "Questions" are sometimes asked to try to make you look bad, revealing flaws in your argument. More often, they are about making the speaker look good, helping him or her display intellect or acumen in front of others. Listen carefully the next time you are in the audience. You'll see what I mean.

There is no correct answer to a statement-question. Indeed, the content of your answer is often irrelevant. What matters is *how* you respond. You need to practice spotting non-questions when they show up and then carefully getting yourself off the hook. Here is a list of the most common varieties, along with suggestions on how to deal with them:

The content of your answer is often irrelevant. What matters is how you respond.

■ **Questions that are clearly statements.** There is always at least one audience member who wants to be heard. His or her question will be along the lines of "I don't think that is the best way to go," followed by an alternative proposal and then "What do you think?" That phrase is the only thing that makes this a question! Also beware of questions that begin or end with "Don't you think?"

The worst thing you can do in response is to get defensive. Instead, take the "high ground" by politely indicating that there are cases to be made for different points of view. If you feel confident, suggest why you think your approach is right. Otherwise, graciously smile and move on. If the person persists with his or her "question," you can suggest taking the question "offline" to discuss later so that you can move on for now.

■ **Questions that are hidden statements.** These are designed to reveal weaknesses or oversights. Often referring to something you haven't mentioned, they may be preceded by a half-compliment to catch you off guard. For example, say you've just presented a new initiative, and someone says, "That was all very interesting, but when will you be bringing on more people for this?" What that question is really saying is that there *should* be additional head count, even though you haven't said so. The question may also be a setup for another statement like "Don't you think we should decide that as a group?"

The trick is to acknowledge but sidestep the question and respond neutrally. Try something like "We are committed to making this work and will bring on additional staff if and when there's a need." This answers the implication beneath the question. It's best never to promise anything in response to a surprise question-statement, but to use a general statement in return.

■ **What-if questions.** These are usually questions about what might go wrong. They are often used to imply that you won't be able to achieve something. "What if you can't complete the project by the deadline?" is an example. Even when they are asked innocently, the best response is, once again, to redirect. In that instance, you might talk about the importance of project timelines and how carefully your team has planned. Since you have been asked a hypothetical question, you need only give a hypothetical answer.

■ **False-facts questions.** When someone asks an inaccurate question such as "Now that you've lost money on this, what can you do to keep costs down?" when you haven't actually lost money, he or she may be trying to show you up. You need to nip any such implication in the bud. Don't get defensive; just politely state the facts—"As a matter of fact, we are on budget"—and move on. If someone wants to argue, you don't have to respond. You've already answered enough. There are times when it's important to just keep moving. If your questioner gets pushy, he or she will simply look bad.

Negotiating statements disguised as questions is not about being in a state of permanent suspicion. It's just about preparing yourself to respond positively, neutrally, or not at all to whatever you're asked, whatever the intent.

TRUTH 35

MEETINGS AND CONFERENCE CALLS ARE KEY OPPORTUNITIES TO MAKE AN IMPRESSION

As you sit down to a meeting, what do you say to yourself? "I can't wait for this to be over" or "What a great opportunity"? More often than not, I imagine it's the former. Many of us see meetings as tedious facts of organizational life, where often little of interest is said and little decided. The real push and pull of work goes on elsewhere.

However, meetings and conference calls (their virtual equivalents) have plenty of plus points. Not only is a well-run meeting a chance to keep groups of colleagues informed and to encourage team spirit, but a meeting of any caliber is an opportunity for you to gain some favorable exposure. Meetings have more impact than one-on-one conversations because you have a bigger audience. Thus, they are good settings to show that you know your stuff by looking and sounding confident in front of peers and superiors.

> *A meeting of any caliber is an opportunity for you to gain some favorable exposure.*

Shining at a meeting or conference call is all about strategic preparation. You think in advance about how you want to come across. And you plan ahead about how you will claim "space" at the table. This preparation is so valuable that it's often worth devoting more time to it than to the meeting itself.

Ask yourself what you want others to say about you after the meeting or call, and prepare questions, anecdotes, and points accordingly. If you want to be known as sharp, bone up on the facts. Strategic? Prepare some what-if questions. Team player? Prepare questions that will draw others and their opinions into the conversation. Interventions need to be more carefully planned for a call than a face-to-face meeting, since there is less room for spontaneity and therefore fewer opportunities to speak. However, you have the advantage of being able to write down exactly what you want to say beforehand, ensuring that your contribution comes across fluently.

Claiming your space at the table, real or virtual, is about announcing and then reinforcing your presence. If the others are not close colleagues, the first thing you should do is identify yourself to them, fixing your name in their heads. On the phone it is doubly important to do that the first time you contribute, because you should never assume that people will recognize your voice. Say your name clearly and confidently so that others can take it in.

Physical tactics can help you assert your presence. When sitting at a table, a strong stance involves keeping your hands visible in the "steeple" position on the table: fingertips touching and facing upward, with your wrists on the tabletop. Focus groups indicate that this conveys a confident presence. When you want to say something, you move your hand forward to "break into" the common space, drawing people's attention to you. A conference call offers no visual clues, so you have to play a slightly different game. Always let the call facilitator know in advance that you want to be called on to contribute, ensuring you an initial launchpad. When you do get to speak, use gestures to help you come across with impact. For example, it can help to punch the air to add a bit of energy as you speak. This would seem eccentric or aggressive in a face-to-face meeting, but it's a secret tool in the world of conference calls.

Canny executives see the frequency and regularity of meetings and conference calls not as a burden but as an opportunity to build and reinforce a positive message about themselves. Follow their example!

TRUTH 36

E-MAIL IS EASY TO USE AND EASY TO ABUSE

E-mail is one of the easiest means of communication available to today's executives. It's also one of the trickiest.

Confused? Well, the thing about e-mail is that its handy nature makes it both easy to use without thinking—leading to misunderstandings over content—and easy to overuse, when other modes of communication might be more appropriate. It's also a form of written communication, meaning that however informal it seems, it sticks around after you write it, making it hard to retract your words. It's therefore worth taking time to consider how to use e-mail effectively. Not only will the quality of your communication improve, but you'll also protect yourself from uncomfortable errors.

The absence of the human factor is one of e-mail's major challenges. E-mail lacks the formalities and niceties, even the handwritten signature, of the letter. This is part of its attraction, in that you can casually knock off e-mails, giving just the facts. However, this direct nature can appear abrupt to some people. And unlike that other, more casual way of communicating—the phone call—there is no tone of voice to make clear the

> *The absence of the human factor is one of e-mail's major challenges.*

spirit of what you are saying, or physical presence to pick up on a listener's puzzlement.

So how can you make e-mail work for you? The following guidelines have been developed over the last decade through trial and error, complaints, and feedback in companies worldwide. Although all are valid, some may be more important than others in different companies. When starting somewhere new, observe the e-mail style of established staff to determine the politeness and norms required.

Follow these suggestions to use e-mail effectively:

- Use a salutation like "Dear" or the recipient's name at the start of each message, and sign off with a brief acknowledgment or thanks.

- Make your message easy to read by keeping sentences short. It's hard to read long sentences on-screen.

- Don't write in all capital letters. This can come across as shouting.

- Take time to read your e-mails before you send them. If the message is an important one, put it to one side in Drafts for a while, and then check it again before sending.

- Reply to e-mails within 24 hours. If you need more time to consider your response, briefly acknowledge the e-mail and let the sender know you will reply soon. Flag messages that still need replies so that you don't forget about them.

■ Don't answer e-mails that you received through a cc. These are for your information only and do not need a reply. Don't waste valuable time on unnecessary acknowledgments.

E-mail is a great tool for acknowledging and disseminating information quickly, for setting up meetings and other complicated arrangements, and for tracking a discussion, particularly when you want to include a number of people. However, there are occasions when you should be wary of it. Avoid e-mail when the contents are confidential or you don't want them to show up in a court of law. E-mails can go astray, and they exist in cyberspace indefinitely. E-mail also is not a good idea when the message has any emotional charge that the reader might misunderstand, when you need to reprimand or even fire someone, or when you're starting a new relationship. In those cases, a phone call or face-to-face conversation creates a much better dynamic.

E-mail is a cheap and convenient means of communication. However, it does have its downsides, so use it to your advantage and with care.

PART VIII

THE TRUTH ABOUT DEALING WITH ENEMIES AND ANTIBODIES

TRUTH 37

IN ALL THINGS, MODERATION: YOU GET BACK WHAT YOU PUT OUT

You've probably heard the expression, "You make your own luck." To a certain extent, that's true. I'm not talking about some new-age idea of karma or fate. It's simply that whatever you do, think, or say has an impact on others that directly determines how those others respond to you. The reaction you get to your words or behaviors usually is similar to what you put out. If you are polite and gracious, for example, you will almost always find that other people behave the same way back to you.

In the same way, strong words and emotions generate strong reactions. At a simple level, if you show strong negative emotions to someone—anger or despair—he or she is likely to respond in a negative way or feel a bit down. Negative thinking is catching. You therefore might think that behaving in a super-positive way would generate very positive reactions. That can happen. But more often than not, in the workplace, where you associate with strangers or people you don't know well, people respond to the strength rather than the mood. Strong positive reactions can overwhelm other people as much as negative ones, prompting them to react defensively, even aggressively, in return. They can feel that you're shouting at them or criticizing them when you're just being enthusiastic.

The thing about strong emotions is that they can get a bit messy. Think of your emotions as a carbonated drink. No one wants a can of soda that explodes and sprays all over them. That's the effect you have when you get overexcited with people by talking quickly, loudly, or in a pushy way. You come across as "overcarbonated." Likewise, if you behave and speak in a completely passionless way, you come across as completely lacking in fizz, or "flat," which is equally undesirable. You need to find a happy medium—to come across as upbeat, or effervescent, like a glass of champagne. A few bubbles encourage others to think about and buy into what you're saying, because you look and sound committed to your ideas.

Think of your emotions as a carbonated drink.

Your choice of words also has considerable impact on how you come across. Once again, avoid strong positive and negative terms, especially when passing judgment on anything. The more neutrally you can describe things to others, the lower the chance of negative reactions. When talking about a sensitive work situation, it can help to think of yourself as a television camera—a tool that objectively captures and describes what lies before it, through the distance of a lens, without criticizing. So when you instinctively want to say, "Our department messed up," it's far wiser to state the facts emotion-free, such as "Four times this year the department has been cited for governance issues." This keeps the general mood calm and neutral, which is far more conducive to working together to sort things out.

TRUTH 38

PLAY YOUR CARDS CLOSE TO YOUR VEST

A "poker face" is the neutral expression gamblers wear when they don't want the other players to know what they're thinking. The phrase "holding your cards close to your vest" comes from the care they take to conceal their cards from the other players' eyes. Used together, these tactics ensure that nothing is given away about the quality of your hand. Even the slightest hint of what you are holding can have a direct influence on the behavior of the other players. If they think you're happy with your cards, they won't bet. But if you show that you're unhappy, they'll bet a lot, knowing they can profit from it.

Holding onto your true feelings is as important for a business professional as it is for a professional poker player.

Holding onto your true feelings is as important for a business professional as it is for a professional poker player. Emotional displays, positive and negative, can create many problems at work. Not only can they make you appear weak or vulnerable, meaning that you are not taken seriously as a corporate player, but they can also create problems for others, making them uncomfortable in your presence or unsure how to respond.

It's not that you shouldn't let others know whether you are happy or unhappy, but you need to be careful about when and how you do so. Keep what you're thinking private until there is an appropriate moment to raise it, and when you do bring it up, do so in a neutral and considered way. Strong emotions of any kind, particularly negative ones, can provoke defensive behavior in others. They may feel that you are trying to push or dominate them, and they might react abrasively in return.

For example, there is nothing wrong with being angry with someone at work for doing something inappropriate. However, that anger should be neither expressed publicly (for the sake of the working atmosphere) nor discussed while it is fresh. It can be more effective to take the other person aside when you have cooled off and calmly and neutrally tell him that his earlier behavior made you unhappy and ask him not to do it again. That way, confrontation is reduced, you appear professional and in control, and your words have much more impact when they aren't wrapped in the "interference" of emotion.

Even if you receive good news—of a wished-for promotion, for example—you should keep positive emotion low-key out of consideration for others. Remember that when somebody wins at work, often somebody else loses out. Obvious happiness may make other people feel bad about themselves and resentful of you. The same goes for praising someone effusively in public. Your happiness with one person's work may make others feel less valued or that they have been ignored or sidelined.

Poker tactics can also protect you from being taken advantage of or pushed around at work. It's worth practicing your poker face—neutral yet not unfriendly—in front of a mirror so that you are ready to look unfazed, whatever anyone says or does. People who bully or tease love reactions, so showing emotion encourages them to bother you again. If you keep your face and body emotion-free, bullies will lose interest. You give them the message that they're not getting to you, even if inside you're upset.

TRUTH 39

DON'T EXPLAIN AND DON'T COMPLAIN: NO ONE LIKES WHINING

There's an old saying: "When someone asks what time it is, he doesn't want to be told how to build a clock." It sounds obvious when put like that. However, it's amazing how many of us, when asked a question, particularly when we are tense and on our guard or keen and eager to please, opt for describing the clock! This trait is something to avoid, particularly in a business environment, where people just want to get things done quickly and efficiently.

Almost nothing annoys people more at work than others explaining or complaining at length. Both activities generate "antibodies"—colleagues whose unfavorable opinion of you can inhibit career progress. People either become irritated or, worse, don't trust you.

Maybe you've seen or heard of the old cop show *Dragnet*, where Sergeant Joe Friday wanted "just the facts." Any bar association course on preparing witnesses stresses the same message: "Less is more." If a witness gives only the key facts, he is seen as believable. But as soon as he starts explaining the detail behind an answer, the less authentic he sounds. Anything beyond simple answers is confusing, or worse, has the look and sound of lying. It isn't the content but the length and level of detail that sounds fishy. It really is like this in business as well. So, whenever you're explaining something, imagine Sergeant Friday there at your ear, asking you for just the facts!

Lengthy complaints work much like lengthy explanations. Both overload listeners and suck energy from the discussion.

Lengthy complaints work much like lengthy explanations. Both overload listeners and suck energy from the discussion. All the extra information detracts from the core message. Not only is this annoying, but it also means that you won't get your point across. For instance, if you want to complain about the faulty coffeemaker, it is far more effective to quickly and clearly explain the problem and suggest a possible solution than to elaborate on the minutiae of the problem and its effects.

Quick and clean complaints and explanations leave no doubt about what the issue is. Others are more likely to listen and to understand what needs doing. You may feel that extra detail paints a clearer picture, but it actually becomes less clear the more you say, since the listener cannot take in everything and has no clear "hook" to grip onto. You actually lose control of your message.

When responding to a question or making a complaint, only give the information that the other person needs to know. You can always ask your own question to clarify what this is. Or you can answer the part of a question you'd most like to answer. Ascertaining the nub of the issue or problem will help you make clear explanations and transform complaints into constructive observations.

What's the key message here? Explaining and complaining at length distort and negate what you're saying so that people stop listening. If someone asks you how you made a decision, you can indicate that you considered a number of alternatives and describe a couple of options but with little detail. The person can ask again if he or she really needs to know. Powerful people don't complain or explain—they get their point across swiftly and succinctly.

TRUTH 40

BE A FORCE FOR THE POSITIVE: IT'S BEST TO BUCK UP WHEN YOU'RE DOWN

Turn off the sound during a tennis match and you can still tell who's winning. The player who slumps her shoulders or grimaces after a bad shot is probably preparing to lose. In contrast, the player who can feel victory within reach just moves calmly on to the next shot, focusing on doing that one well and putting the mistake behind her.

When you make a mistake at work, it's important not to focus on the error, but to channel your energy into bouncing back.

When you make a mistake at work, it's equally important not to focus on the error, but to channel your energy into bouncing back. This isn't only about keeping yourself on the winning path, but others too, since in an intense environment, emotions are contagious. An upbeat attitude, when not overdone, can become a major force, because the positive energy hits people as something they want to follow or aspire to. They'll soon forget about the mistake if you do, and they will maintain an overriding impression of you as a winner and those you work with as the winning team.

It's not that you don't pay attention to what has gone wrong. What you do is look at what happened and learn from it quickly. It's the learning that counts. Or, rather than learn from the mistake or problem, you "cherish" it. This means thinking about it from all sides and considering the various factors that interplayed to bring it about. That way, you don't end up making the same mistake again. Seeing it as a positive force for learning, as opposed to a negative setback, helps you put it behind you.

The key to managing a problem or mistake is compartmentalizing it. It's a little like a puppy that poops in the wrong spot. Walking away from the mess is a way to quickly get back into the rhythm of your job. Once you've learned something, there is no need to keep thinking about what went wrong. The negative is put to one side. Even a bit of denial helps you move on, as long as you don't openly put the blame on someone else.

Whining and complaining never help since they tend to bring you and others down. Once a negative thought is expressed, it gets even stronger and can literally suck energy from your colleagues. That doesn't mean that you don't publicly admit your mistakes. It does mean that you don't dwell on them.

Mistakes are great learning opportunities as long as you manage them. The first way to manage them is to think in advance about what might possibly go wrong and to prepare Plans B and C. The second way is to avoid repeating the same mistakes. It's not so terrible to make a mistake once. It's a consequence of trying new ideas and approaches. Nothing ventured, nothing gained.

Most great leaders and companies have a large mistake in their past, but rarely the same mistake twice. Candy king Milton Hershey, known to anyone who likes chocolate, went bankrupt with an early company but persevered. Although Richard Branson said that he wanted his company, Virgin, to be as well known around the world as Coca-Cola, he couldn't get his brand of cola off the ground. Since he has had major successes with other businesses, he ignored that setback.

The power of positive thinking is not only the name of a book; it's a way of life. A realistic degree of positive optimism will help you be successful in spite of setbacks and will make you a good person to be around.

TRUTH 41

A TEFLON TEMPERAMENT IS
THE BEST ARMOR

Ronald Reagan, genial and ever-smiling, was known as the Teflon president. With a personality that enabled him to ignore unpleasant facts, he conveyed a positive view of the future no matter what happened. Bad news didn't stick to him since he didn't react to it. Whatever they thought of his politics, most Americans admired President Reagan's style.

The working day is full of opportunities to get hot and bothered, from the minor frustrations of e-mail not working to the major setback of someone else getting your promotion. Acquiring a Teflon temperament, like the late president's, is a surefire way to stay cool, whatever life throws at you. Bad stuff rolls off you so quickly that you don't even know it's there. The good news is that even if you're not cool,

With focus and practice you can build your Teflon coating and insulate yourself from conflict and negativity at work.

calm, and collected by nature, with focus and practice you can build your Teflon coating and insulate yourself from conflict and negativity at work.

Acquiring a Teflon temperament is partly a mind trick; the coating is something to visualize in your mind and imagine yourself putting on each morning as you walk into the office. You then remind yourself of its presence each time you enter a challenging situation or conversation. In contrast to an imagined suit of armor, with its connotations of battle and defensiveness and its restrictive form, your imagined Teflon is just a thin invisible coating that effortlessly insulates you from strife.

It's amazing how powerful an act of imagination a Teflon coating can be. It's the visual equivalent of counting to 10 when something angers or upsets you. Although with Teflon you learn to stop the frustration from getting through in the first place by establishing a distance from it. Once you distance yourself from an issue, you can be dispassionate and think in a calm and positive way about what to do next. The distance and positive attitude are key. Contrary to popular thinking about letting it all hang out, expressing negative views can actually affect you negatively, limiting your ability to respond with energy and creativity. Teflon helps you take an objective and positive view of what's possible.

Few Teflon temperaments are 100 percent impermeable. From time to time holes appear and frustrations bubble through. You limit the likelihood of this happening by keeping yourself relaxed and stress-free. This is helped by really basic practical stuff such as making sure you get enough sleep, eating and drinking properly, taking part in regular exercise, and practicing stress-reduction techniques such as meditation or deep breathing. Set aside breaks during your workday to rest your mind and body, even if it's just a short walk to the other end of the office and back. If something gets through your Teflon, taking a 15-minute time-out in that way can help you get back on course.

Stepping back from a difficult situation is the key to creating positive thinking and objectivity. Demonstrating these qualities will show others that you are senior management material. When you are under stress, a Teflon temperament is a handy ace to have up your sleeve. Bring it into play every time you have to face something difficult.

PART IX

THE TRUTH ABOUT MAKING THE RIGHT IMPRESSION

TRUTH 42

THINK CENTRAL CASTING:
LOOKING THE PART MATTERS

"Central Casting" is a Hollywood department that keeps head shots of available actors. These range from people who look like "everyman" or "everywoman," ideal to play typical family members, to those resembling archetypal doctors or lawyers. Central Casting decides at a glance what type of part an actor suits, filing the photos accordingly. For an aspiring star, it's a whole lot easier to get the role you want if you look the part, rather than convincing a director to cast against type.

The same goes for the aspiring executive. The less work you have to do to convince an employer or client that you are right for the job, the better. One of the easiest things you can do is look the part. However talented you are, if you don't look like a professional, manager, or leader, others may, rightly or wrongly, not see you as one. This is true whether you are applying for a position or are already in the role you want but hope to be taken seriously.

Take the story of the "chief geek" of a well-known U.S. cell phone company. As one of the top executives in her field, this woman has the ear of senior management and the respect of the workforce. However, despite exceptional ability, her path to the top was not an easy one. After a bright debut, she ended up stuck at mid-management level in her late 30s, failing to gain the desired promotion.

So what changed? The executive realized that the one thing she wasn't doing was playing the part she wanted. Slender and petite, dressed in soft skirts and blouses, she just hadn't been "reading" as a powerful executive. As soon as she understood this, she started to wear the uniform of the executive corps—bold colors and suits with shoulder pads—and people started to see her differently. Our heroine rapidly progressed, securing her dream job before she turned 50.

Anyone can apply her techniques:

■ **Look the part through investment dressing.** Observe the styles and colors favored by senior executives of your gender, and use that as a guide. A good suit, in the right colors for you, is generally a wise investment. There's something about the construction of suits that just adds to personal impact. For men, normal colors are dark blue and gray, both of which project authority and trustworthiness. For women, there's less of a formula, so observation of others is key. Black and blue are "safe" colors but make you blend in. A small or shy woman can augment her impact with bold shades. A confident or larger woman might consider wearing her eye color or a more muted shade.

> *Observe the styles and colors favored by senior executives of your gender, and use that as a guide.*

■ **Look the part with grooming and accessories.**
Neatness counts. For men, facial hair should follow
company norms unless you want to make a statement
of individuality. Regular haircuts will keep you from
looking shaggy. For women, hair should be becoming
but not distracting. Avoid striking jewelry and scarves
unless you're in an industry that appreciates such flair,
such as fashion or media.

Never forget that you are acting on the corporate stage
and playing a part that is an authentic part of you, but not all
of you. Prepare as an actor does to love the part and believe
that you *are* that part. Looking right is the first step.

TRUTH 43

SOUNDING THE PART MATTERS TOO!

In the 2004 U.S. presidential election, one big difference between the two candidates was the way in which they presented their ideas. These contrasting approaches became known as "Bush-speak" and "Kerry-speak."

"Bush-speak" consists of short sentences of five to eight words, using few "buts," "ands," "howevers," and other verbal clutter. Communication experts represent "Bush-speak" as a straight line: sentences that are easy for listeners to understand and remember.

"Kerry-speak" is much more complex. He pauses, includes different perspectives, and thinks about what he is saying, circling back to add additional ideas. Communication experts represent "Kerry-speak" as a spiral: sentences that are harder to remember since the message is not simple.

Who won? That's right: Bush. Elections are not won on presentation style alone, but you can bet Bush's speeches played a part in his success. Research has shown that short, simple sentences, spoken without hesitation, make a speaker seem in control of a situation, sure of himself and his opinions—the kind of qualities we associate with, and want in, a leader.

These are therefore the qualities you want others in the workplace to associate with you. By contrast, long sentences can sound unsure, tentative, and weak—not desirable leadership qualities.

Tone and volume are important too. Short, precise sentences and a low-pitched but clearly audible voice make a powerful combination. Together they add up to the classic leader sound, known as "command tone." Generals, principals, and police all have it, and everyone knows that they are in charge. Sounding like them can help you get the roles and responsibilities you want.

Short, simple sentences make a speaker seem in control. Long sentences can sound unsure, tentative, and weak.

Work on making your voice a tone lower by thinking of the sound emerging from inside your lungs rather than your throat. Or spend time breathing from your abdomen and relaxing your neck muscles before an important event. Such exercises are particularly important for younger women, whose higher-pitched voices may work against their ability and experience.

Moving your voice down at the end of sentences, rather than up in a questioning style, also displays confidence. A rising tone tends to imply uncertainty or a request for permission. It may be suitable for a kindergarten teacher offering milk and cookies to a child, but it is not the sound of a leader.

Projecting your voice so that everyone in the room can hear you, but without shouting, can be practiced with a friend or colleague in a conference or meeting room. Without raising the pitch of your voice, speak so that someone on the other side of the room can hear you. Imagine your voice reaching the far wall. Not loud enough? Think beyond the walls and out into the street. But keep your body relaxed and your voice in your lungs.

You learn to sound like a leader by practicing in similar low-risk environments, or even when you're at home. Honing your technique when you're not in the hot seat means that you don't have to think about it when you are. The astronauts who first walked on the moon practiced so much that actually being on the moon was "just like practice" for them. Following their example will help you reduce the stress of important presentations or meetings.

Remember that initial impressions persist. When speaking with a key boss, client, or associate, particularly for the first time, you need to come across as confident and experienced. The way you sound plays a big part in this.

TRUTH 44

MIND YOUR MANNERS!

When Aretha Franklin sang "R-E-S-P-E-C-T," most everyone identified with it. Somehow, though, when we want to make something happen at work, in our haste or enthusiasm we may forget all about those seven letters. In fact, the number one catalyst for Equal Employment Opportunity Commission hearings is the *way* in which an ex-employee was treated when terminated. Respect is the issue.

Respect may seem a rather old-fashioned concept, something shown to the high-school principal and mafia dons, or something to do with the shady world of office politics, and thus rejected as an "unmentionable" in our equal-opportunity, merit-focused workplaces. Indeed, in the past, respect was largely reserved for one's "betters." However, it is important to remember that, in life and at work, *all* people want to be treated respectfully—to believe that they, and what they do, matter.

Respect, shown in all directions, is certainly not an outdated idea, and can reap dividends. It defuses negativity and lubricates organizational wheels. In the short term, respect may smooth your career path and open doors for you. In the longer term, it encourages workplace harmony, helping people work better together. Respect at work builds loyalty, stability, and sustainable business processes.

You might think that for such major impact you would have to invest a fair bit of time and energy. On the contrary, it is easy, with simple gestures and acknowledgments, to become known as a person who considers others and values their contributions. It's often just a question of good manners. This doesn't mean reading and remembering a big book of etiquette, but it does mean consistently being polite and patient; saying hello, please, and thank you; and paying attention to basic courtesies like remembering names and titles, particularly when you are with people from outside the U.S. Americans are sometimes much less formal than the rest of the world.

I'm always surprised when people think they don't have time for manners at work, especially when dealing with support staff. Indeed, the lower someone's job grade, the more gracious and kind you should be. Your gestures will be appreciated, and favors will be returned in unexpected ways. You never know what the future will hold. Those lowly assistants may rise to positions of power and influence and will remember the kindness you showed them.

In contrast, individuals who see themselves as slighted by you can react by causing trouble in more subtle ways, acting as "antibodies" in your working life as they try to get back at you or the company. Legal retaliation is an extreme reaction, but resentful people may try to put obstacles in your way or refuse to do more than the bare minimum for you. So, be polite and courteous to everyone no matter how you feel about them; it never pays to make an enemy at work.

In the hustle and bustle of business, we often forget to acknowledge the contributions others make. But nothing could be simpler than saying or sending a gracious thank-you to those who go out of their way to make your working life easier. Your actions go a long way toward getting others onboard. Displays of manners and respect show that you are

Displays of manners and respect show that you are capable of assuming a higher-level position and moving ahead.

capable of assuming a higher-level position and moving ahead in your company. Those who matter will notice.

TRUTH 45

EXITS AND ENTRANCES MATTER

Williiam Shakespeare wrote:

All the world's a stage,
And all the men and women merely players.
They have their exits and entrances,
And one man in his time plays many parts...

Exits and entrances are key moments not only in theater but also in life, just as Shakespeare's words suggest. People tend to remember beginnings and endings more than what happens in the middle. This is true not only of drama performances, but of the roles you perform on the corporate stage. How you move into and out of jobs has an enormous impact on perceptions of your success, since these are the times when colleagues and bosses may notice your every move. The more important the part, the

As you move into and out of jobs, colleagues and bosses are more likely to notice your every move.

more you are observed. And observations made at these moments tend to endure.

Many of us forget that to move on to a new role we need to let go of what went before. Exiting a job well is about ensuring that your successor is in the loop, included in key meetings and correspondence, and prepared enough to be able to step smoothly into your place. It is not about doing every bit of paperwork and tying up every loose end. Although it's important to move forward in an orderly way, it's even more important to know when to leave behind your old role and expertise. For someone who has been highly successful, this can be hard. You have to forget that you're the best at something and move to a new place of uncertainty.

William Bridges, guru of management transitions, describes the moment of leaving the old and starting something new as shifting into the "neutral zone." This can be a shaky period as you are under pressure to make a good first impression. The urge is to get moving, or to "hit the ground running." Bad idea. The "neutral zone" is your time to ready yourself: to gather resources, support, and information from all constituencies and key players to show that you can listen and to build your vision for the future.

Taking the time to make a comfortable transition is not about doing nothing. It's about observing the lay of the land and considering options for future moves or changes. This involves really listening to your new staff and colleagues and noticing their needs. If you can identify temporary solutions to help people be more effective, or resolve nagging issues, you can make these happen. But give yourself a "get-out clause" by stressing their temporary nature as a stopgap until you are up to speed. Staying neutral for a period of months to gather views, news, concerns, and challenges may not be as fun or energizing as action, but it allows you to develop your thinking and strategy for long-term impact. Entrances are high-profile moments in your career.

Think of this time of transition as an orderly passing of the baton in a relay race. You take care to synchronize your pace with your teammate when it is time for you to take the baton and move into the race. Then, when you need to exit, you don't stop running as you pass the baton, but you do step back from the race once the baton is passed.

TRUTH 46

YOUR WORK SPACE REFLECTS WHO YOU ARE (AND WHO YOU WANT TO BE)

It may be that you can't tell a book by its cover. However, you can tell a lot about someone by going into his or her work space, office, or cubicle. Every feature, right down to the placement of papers on the desk, sends a message about who you are and how you do things.

Whether you like it or not, others interpret your work area as a reflection of your personality and thinking. It's the one physical environment where you really leave your mark in the workplace; all other spaces are just borrowed for the duration of a meeting or conversation. It's therefore important, however trivial a matter it might seem on the surface, to take time to ensure that your work space reflects you in a positive light. Take the opportunity to convey not just a message about who you are, but about who you aspire to be. From the décor or knickknacks to the very papers on your desk, everything about your work space needs to say that you are a professional and that you are going places.

Décor is an area in which to tread carefully. While judicious use of personal pictures can show you to be a family person, team player, or motivated character—"Here I am on top of

Cute screensavers, cuddly toys, and an excess of plants can detract from your professionalism.

Everest"—cute screensavers, cuddly toys, and an excess of plants can detract from your professionalism. It isn't that self-expression is bad, but in the small area of a work space, each item becomes more noticeable, taking on greater significance as a symbol of who you are. Some companies even have in-house stipulations about what can and can't be put on your desk. At Oracle, for example, only one personal item is allowed, meaning that what you choose to display takes on even more significance.

You can use the limited space or any enforced limitations to your advantage by choosing décor items specifically to act as conversation starters. A popular book, judiciously placed, just like that Everest photo, could draw the attention of someone significant passing by and initiate a useful relationship. Think not only about what your chosen objects say about you, but what others might find to say about them.

Clutter of any kind is to be avoided, particularly messy piles of paper. It sends a powerful message, functioning as a kind of "noise" that distracts others from your capabilities. Not only does clutter create a metaphorical barrier between you and others—suggesting that your mind is not quite on the shared business—but if it gets really bad, it becomes a physical barrier. When someone comes to see you, he or she usually sits or stands near your desk. Any piles of papers are between you and your visitor. They are distracting even if arranged neatly.

I'm not talking about the "clean desk every night" club. Too tidy a desk may suggest that you can't cope with too many projects at once. There's nothing wrong with a bit of disarray, particularly if you're in the middle of a project. In the short term, this says, "I'm terribly busy and devoted to this important project." But what if you have a lot of projects at the same time? Those papers can quickly get out of hand. The trick is to organize them in file boxes on your desk or on a shelf. With the messy side turned inward, the effect is a bit like a row of books. The papers aren't so obvious but are easily accessible. This is particularly effective, even essential, with anything that is at all proprietary or confidential.

Paying attention to your work space is a simple way to show yourself off to best advantage. Your desk, cubicle, or office is more than a work space and filing cabinet. It's a stage on which you can perform to the level of your aspirations.

PART X

THE TRUTH
ABOUT GETTING
NOTICED

TRUTH 47

EVERY PRESENTATION IS AN OPPORTUNITY FOR YOU TO SHINE

At the tender age of 16, a young man named William Hague made a speech at his political party's conference in the UK. Despite his youth, he knocked the audience's socks off. Twenty years later, that young man became the youngest leader of the Conservative party of Great Britain in over 200 years. Hague had carefully built on that initial day in the spotlight.

In any organization, exposure is the key to getting known and getting ahead. Speeches and presentations are among the best ways to put yourself out there. However, like any public exposure, risk is involved: If your moment in the spotlight goes badly, your reputation can be permanently damaged. You minimize risk, and maximize potential glory, through careful preparation.

In any organization, exposure is the key to getting known and getting ahead.

Preparation isn't just about knowing your subject, although that is certainly important. The real key to success is to prepare for your audience and their expectations, determining in advance what you want to leave them with so that you can tailor every aspect of your presentation to that end. Think about how you want to come across, not just through the words you use, but through how you look, how you use your face and body, and how you respond to questions. The less familiar the group, the more you should prepare. For a major event, it's not excessive to commit one hour of preparation for every minute of presentation.

Here are some of the things you might want your audience to say after you have given a presentation, and how to get the audience to say them:

- **You know your stuff and are on top of the issues.** You come across as an expert when you present your ideas clearly and logically. Your audience feels convinced by you when they can follow your argument, so lay a clear thread or theme for them through your points. Slides can be useful props to keep you on track, but put only triggers on them, not everything you want to say, or your audience will focus on reading them and will stop listening to you. However much you love your topic, resist the temptation to tell the audience everything. Keep it focused and short; three major points are about the most people can remember.

- **You're someone to be listened to.** You come across as authoritative when you dress and speak like a professional. Professionals dress one level above their audience; if the audience is dressed casually, you need to wear business attire. You also command respect when you cite the thoughts and opinions of senior management. Even if you haven't spoken with them personally, your references can imply a personal association.

- **You answer their questions.** You meet questions with confidence by ascertaining likely ones and then addressing your speech toward them. Either talk to audience members in advance to find out what they want to know, or find out from their staff what matters to them. With an important group, it's worth asking colleagues to do a practice run with you.

- **You keep your cool under pressure.** You impress people when you handle difficult questions well, shrugging them off with good humor, deflecting any antagonistic questions with a neutral response, or calmly and confidently admitting that you don't know the answer but will find out what it is. Failing technology can offer you a chance to gain some glory if you respond with initiative and sangfroid. Be ready for your slides not to work, for example, and be happy to talk without them.

TRUTH 48

EVERYONE HAS HIS OR HER STORY ON THE STREET

As teenagers we start to learn about, and care about, our reputations: our "story on the street." How others perceive us, in the neighborhood or at school, starts to matter, influencing our behavior as well as the peer groups we choose. Such realization, even redefinition, of identity is a fundamental stage of adolescence. We may come to realize how wrong or one-sided the story that's told about us can be, compared to how we feel about ourselves. The high school "jock" may actually be the most shy guy in the class deep down.

Although it may become less of a daily preoccupation, the fact that we have a story on the street does not go away with age. In every place you work you will have one, and it will affect how your coworkers perceive you. You may know part of this story, but rarely all, because some things will never be said to your face! It spreads each time someone talks about you at work and when others

If you get angry about something in a meeting early on, you may be labeled "emotional."

repeat parts of what they hear. Once a certain story takes hold, it can be hard to shake. Get angry about something in a meeting once early on, for example, and you may be labeled an "emotional" person for the foreseeable future. That's why it's worth both being aware or, and taking control of, your reputation.

The good news is that you have the power to fundamentally influence your story. Far from being a passive bystander in its creation, you can actually help write it. It's your job to "frame" who you are. One great early story-shaper was Queen Elizabeth I, who called herself the "Virgin Queen." History suggests she almost certainly wasn't. Nonetheless, she said it often enough that British schoolchildren still repeat her story 500 years later.

Keep these three main tactics in mind when taking control of your personal story at work:

- **Tell others what you stand for.** Decide what you want to be known for in your organization, and make sure that this is what you mention when you meet, greet, or do business with anyone important—and, ideally, anyone at all. (The more people you can get to tell the story your way, the better.) A clear message, repeated often, helps others remember you and what you stand for. If you want to be known for how commercially minded you are, for example, you need to talk about money-making or leveraging business at every opportunity.

- **Be aware of how you and your words come across to others.** It's not just what you say, but how you say it. You can never be entirely sure how people will interpret the "how" of your utterances. If you are passionate about what you are saying, for instance, it can come across as intense or aggressive, and you may consequently be tagged that way. So give some thought to your tone, volume, and speed of voice and the impressions they generate, particularly when you are caught unawares. One quick but forceful reaction can shape a story all too swiftly and strongly.

■ **Make sure that others are aware of your activities and achievements.** The perceived nature of your performance is a third component of your story on the street. When you do a great job or make lots of money and it looks too easy, others may think you did it with smoke and mirrors or that you're just lucky. You certainly should not moan and groan about how hard you're working, but you do need to make your strategy and tactics clear so that you and your team get the credit you deserve.

Time spent thinking about what you want your story to be, and time that you dedicate to generating that storyline, always pays off. Every day offers another opportunity to shape your story in the company's conversation grapevine.

TRUTH 49

HOW YOU MOVE SUGGESTS YOUR POSITION IN THE COMPANY

Although the days of aristocratic masters and humble servants have largely disappeared, some remnants linger in how people, often unconsciously, behave with others they believe to be inferior or superior to themselves. It's important to be aware of how these behaviors can affect how you are perceived at work. The impression we make on others has a subliminal component. When you act like a servant, even in small ways, others may think of you as one.

When you act like a servant, even in small ways, others may think of you as one.

Servants react quickly, highly responsive to the needs of their employers. They may even jump up and run in response to requests. At work, there are employees who move like that. If you're one of them, you probably don't see it as a bad thing. You may even have been praised for your behavior. You're likely to be a highly conscientious and committed person whom others can count on to get the job done. The problem is that the very speed with which you get things done can make you look like a servant, not someone destined for a position of authority. It's even worse when you rush physically. If you want to get ahead at work, you need to learn how to respond in a professional and timely way and not move too fast.

What does not "moving too fast" look like in practice?

- **When answering the phone.** To begin with, there are small yet significant things like not answering the phone on the first ring. A quick pickup can suggest that you are sitting by the phone waiting to receive orders. Holding off until the second or third ring gives the message that you have other preoccupations on your mind.

- **When responding to e-mails.** Likewise, don't get others accustomed to instant replies. Unless they're urgent, draft your answers and then put them aside to send at the end of the day. It's not about keeping people waiting; you're just making it clear that you have things of your own to get on with.

- **When completing assignments.** The same logic should be applied to any projects you work on. Again, there's no need to drag your feet. Just don't rush to complete if there's no pressure to do so. Plan your work so that you can calmly complete the assignment within the allotted time. That way, people see you as dependable and competent, but they implicitly understand that they can't take advantage of your good nature to make unreasonable demands.

When starting a new job, you can send out the message that you are in control from the start. It's more challenging when you want to change the habits of a lifetime in an existing position. Even though you're still performing above average, people may notice the slower responses. Preempt this by informing people that you have a big rush of work on and will be pacing yourself more. They may be disappointed, but they can't accuse you of slack behavior.

People who are in control of their own working lives move in a thoughtful and measured way. As you move into more senior roles, you need to work on perfecting that executive speed while still delivering the good results that got you there. People will respect you for it.

TRUTH 50

IF YOU WANT IT TO BE REMEMBERED, PUT IT IN WRITING

Thomas Paine, a frustrated English tax officer, moved to the American colonies in 1774. As he tapped into the revolutionary spirit of the times, life took on new meaning. Paine started to articulate some of the interesting ideas he came across through writing pamphlets. He challenged the men of the 13 colonies to stop being "summer soldiers and sunshine patriots" and to revolt against taxation without representation. The pamphlets were so popular that they were read by a greater percentage of the population than today watch the Super Bowl. Paine inspired George Washington's army to get out there and fight for their rights.

Today we don't use pamphlets to send out the word. We use e-mails, reports, articles, slides, and flip charts. But the impact and lesson remain the same. Putting your ideas in writing gets your message noticed and remembered far more than if you just spoke about it. Not only that, but writing things down helps crystallize thought by forcing you to clearly articulate ideas and opinions. Painful as it can be to mold those sparks and flashes of ideas in your head into neat letters, words, and phrases, the act of doing so can give you, and your readers, something solid and easy to remember to focus hearts and minds.

Putting thoughts and discussions into writing ensures that good ideas don't get lost in the shuffle. When you're in a meeting or discussion at work, lots of great ideas get tossed around. Unless they become action items and get written down, they quickly fade into the background. It's easy to forget or misremember what was said. For all intents and purposes, if it's not in the minutes or meeting notes, it didn't happen. It's therefore in your best interests, if you're on a conference call or at a meeting where the outcome matters to you, to ask that minutes be taken. If no official administrator is present, you may even want to consider writing and circulating the minutes yourself.

Lots of great ideas get tossed around in a meeting. Unless they become action items and get written down, they quickly fade.

Paine discovered that simply written words, especially when written with passion and commitment, can bring people together around common principles as they are passed from person to person. A shared reference point is established, giving firm foundations on which to build future collective action. So if you want to see something happen at work, rather than just bringing it up with colleagues or moaning at the water cooler, take time to set it down as a discussion document, or rustle up a few slides to show at the next strategy meeting. People then start taking that idea seriously. They also remember much more of what they see than what they hear.

Another good reason for writing things down is that it allows your ideas to go places you can't. If you do get around to typing up that discussion document or white paper, somebody might pass it to somebody else important, who might just like the ideas and start paying attention to you in a way that he or she wouldn't have done otherwise.

One caveat, though: Writing is so memorable that you need to be careful what you write. Be absolutely sure that your thoughts won't embarrass you or your company. You can't take back that document once it's out there. But if you do want people to talk about your ideas, put them in writing!

PART XI

THE TRUTH ABOUT GETTING AHEAD

TRUTH 51

IT'S YOUR JOB TO PROVE THAT YOU'RE READY FOR THE NEXT LEVEL

You've been in your job three years: It's time to move up. Sounds right, doesn't it? Wrong. There are very few jobs left where you move up by virtue of time in the job. Today's company wants to know if you have had three years of progressively more complex and responsible experiences or just had the same year of experience three times.

Take the case of a state supreme court judge in Oklahoma who was upset at not being voted chief state justice by his peers. He thought his decades of experience and proven reputation would trump any other candidate, securing his promotion. However, he forgot that a judge, who essentially runs his individual business, needs different abilities to those of a chief justice, who has to coordinate others in a team. In his case, and in yours,

Identifying and cultivating skills that matter at the next level is more important than being great at your current job.

identifying and cultivating skills that matter at the next level is far more important than being great at those used in the present one.

If you want to be promoted, it is your responsibility, and no one else's, to ensure that you gain experiences and develop skills that will benefit you at the next level. Take every chance to develop the necessary skills. Then, when you feel it's time to move, it's your job, once again, to draw attention to your abilities. Help others realize how much you have progressed by looking for opportunities to try out your extended talents. You need to do this without diminishing those of others; making yourself look good should never be about making others look bad.

Proving that you think and act like someone at the next level is often the clincher. Here are some ways you might take the initiative to do that:

- **Put yourself in your boss's shoes.** Do some homework to find out what your boss is currently concerned about, and look for ways to assist her with her objectives. You might gather popular support for an initiative, for example, showing that you can both network and unify people.

- **Write a "white paper"—a thought piece** on what matters for your department or function, now or in the future. Circulate this to key decision-makers. It will both stimulate their thinking and act as evidence that you think at a higher level.

- **Develop a discussion document to circulate outside your area,** requesting input on an initiative.

It doesn't have to be fancy; bullet points work just fine. Present the resulting ideas and consensus openly, crediting all involved. This not only generates buy-in but also shows that you can work with other groups.

- **Identify obstacles that prevent your team being as effective as it could be.** What would it take to remove these? Circulate ideas for solutions, laying out potential costs and consequences. You don't have to offer a definitive answer, but offer viable suggestions for further discussion.

- **Look for opportunities to join a task force or project team** about a pressing issue. Just asking that you be considered for one shows that you are thinking more broadly about the business's needs. If you can lead or even initiate one, all the better.

- Last but not least, **make sure that there is someone to take over your old duties.** Maybe it's time to coach and guide your successor for the job you're in now. Then there's one less excuse for not letting you move on.

TRUTH 52

THE FEEL-GOOD FACTOR FOSTERS COMMITMENT FROM OTHERS

When Lyndon B. Johnson was in the U.S. Senate, he used to tell mentors like Sam Rayburn and Franklin Roosevelt, "You're just like a daddy to me." In his homey Texas way, LBJ associated himself with a "feel-good factor": Because his mentors felt good about themselves when they were with him, they felt good about him too. It's as simple as that.

I call this behavior "paying homage." This may sound like a rather antiquated concept—the type of thing people do to kings and queens and in history books. However, it is important to realize that today's business office is no less full of hierarchies and allegiances than the courts of yesteryear, and it is in your best interests to observe and respect these. In the contemporary workplace, that's not just about attending to those above you, but treating your colleagues and those who report to you with respect too.

Paying homage is not about being insincere or sycophantic, but about making others feel good about themselves and what they do for you, whether they are a boss or an employee, and their associating that feeling with you. It's telling people how they helped you or the business, paying careful attention to someone's point of view, or simply thanking people sincerely for services rendered. It's an important skill for everyone, whatever your level in the hierarchy.

Paying homage is about making others feel good about themselves and what they do for you and their associating that feeling with you.

Politicians understand how important paying homage is. Businesspeople can learn a lot from them. My mother once met John F. Kennedy, and she never forgot that moment. His focus and listening skills were so amazing that he made her feel as if she were the only person in the room. Bill Clinton has a similar reputation. Such ability to really see and hear another person is exceptional; others want to follow those who possess it. When a colleague tells you how much he or she enjoyed meeting someone, that person was probably paying homage, consciously or not.

So how do you become one of those people? Look for chances to let key contacts know the positives of your experiences with them, such as when they've done a good job, said something interesting, or supported you in some way. Give specifics whenever you can so that they know why you think they're good. Remembering people's names and small details about them—such as holiday destinations—is always appreciated. However, avoid obsequious behavior by giving praise or attention only where it is due. For instance, if you have enjoyed a speech, you might compliment the speaker on it. It works best to compliment something specific like the organization or the speech's impact rather than giving a general compliment.

Paying homage is about making the effort to outwardly express genuine thoughts and feelings, not faking them. Most people can spot sycophants. Bear in mind that it's easier to pay homage in person than in writing. Sometimes a casual comment looks over the top when written down. Paying homage in small amounts, but often and irregularly, seems to work best.

Skilled homage-payers are easy to be with, show appreciation, and help others feel good about themselves. There's nothing old-fashioned about that!

TRUTH 53

LIKEABILITY MEANS LEVERAGE

In order to be persuasive, it is also helps to be likeable. In fact, according to the Gallup poll, likeability has been the one single element that has been absolutely and positively correlated to predicting the winner since 1975.

Let's be clear. Likeability is not about being super-funny or the life of the party. It's not about winning the office popularity contest. Likeable people are just those who are comfortable and easy to be with and who treat others fairly and politely. These character traits bring down others' defenses, making them feel comfortable in your presence, and happy to give you their time and attention. It's then easier to get what you want from them, since they will be looking for ways to affirm that connection.

> **Likeable people are comfortable and easy to be with and treat others fairly and politely.**

Consider two people vying for a promotion. One is young and inexperienced. Friendly and honest, he has a genuine commitment to people's well-being and a tendency toward positive thinking. People really enjoy working with him. The other is an experienced, highly effective manager of large teams. She is smart, tough, and pedantic and likes to outline the worst-case scenario to get people moving.

Who gets the job? It's likely that the younger contender will triumph. Management may well decide that it would be easier to teach the inexperienced executive some management skills than to try to change the interpersonal skills of the more experienced employee.

The younger manager in this example may have natural charm, but he also is a canny player. He knows which workplace behaviors bring others over to his side by making them feel appreciated and important. Even if you don't see yourself as charismatic or gregarious, you can follow his example and increase your likeability simply by making time and space to empathize with others' needs and concerns rather than always seeing the world from your own perspective.

In fact, those are the fundamental qualities of likeability: empathy and consideration for others. The worst thing you can do, if you want people to like you, is to focus your energies on trying to be likeable. The character Willy Loman, in Arthur Miller's classic *Death of a Salesman*, tries too hard to be "well liked" and never achieves his goal. If you do the same, others will perceive you as needy and smell your desperation. In contrast, you should focus your energies outward and concentrate on smoothing the way so that others feel good about themselves when they're with you. Then the likeability just comes naturally. Make sure that you listen well and allocate time for talking one on one with colleagues and junior staff. Be careful not to lecture people or to try to show how smart you are. Keep your words and behavior low-key. It's those quiet and subtle but caring and committed actions that make the difference.

Other people's opinions have a big impact on your working life. The more you're liked by others, the easier it is to get their votes, whether you're a TV performer, a political candidate, or an executive.

TRUTH 54

WORK IS A GAME—AND ONE WORTH PLAYING WELL

Sports analogies are used every day in organizations. We may not be baseball stars, but we still "go to bat" for people when we show support, "step up to the plate" when accepting responsibility, and "strike out" when we fail to do something. American football comes into play when our boss "runs interference" for us, or when we take out the opposition.

Besides the slang, there are more fundamental commonalities between organizational and sporting life. Like many a team activity, work is a game with rules of its own. Don't let the term "game" deceive you, however; work is not about play. It is a defined terrain within which recognized strategies are played out, resulting in winners and losers. If you

> *Like many a team activity, work is a game with rules of its own.*

want to be on the winning side, you need to be a "team player," representing others in a positive light. And you need to play within the rules of the game, making sure that you stay on the field and don't go out of bounds. Take pleasure in getting to know those rules, and work on improving your strategies every day, just as you would your tennis swing or goal kick.

There are ideal playing fields for behavior in all organizations: unwritten definitions of what is considered appropriate and effective in terms of both performance and interpersonal activity. Expectations vary from organization to organization, influenced by culture and location—especially those of headquarters. A company based in New York City has different norms than one based in Atlanta or London. For instance, the way people talk with each other may be more direct in New York companies.

How do you know you're playing within the bounds? By getting feedback, good and tough, all the time. Your boss— your organizational coach—is often the best gauge. Pay attention to his or her criticism and guidance, or make a point of asking for regular appraisals if you don't get these automatically. Sports figures get their weekly statistics, or weekly feedback. Although some behaviors, like lying and cheating, are clearly out of line, many other small, unconscious habits can get in the way of good performance without your realizing that you have a problem.

Take Sam. The otherwise highly regarded employee of a Fortune 50 company, Sam had the damaging habit of making sarcastic remarks to colleagues. He would say things like "You've got a snowball's chance in hell of pulling this one out" to a coworker struggling with a difficult project. Sam was shocked when his boss told him that he was in danger of getting sidelined because of his interpersonal style, so he immediately began acting super-nice to change people's perceptions. He worked so hard to change that he ended up bouncing from one extreme to another, making other people suspicious as well as offended!

His boss then helped Sam understand what was appropriate. He needed to stay neutral to positive in his treatment of people. Sam knew that he was learning when he found himself hesitating as he started to say something sarcastic. He even corrected himself by explaining, "I'm a recovering curmudgeon." His playing field looked like this:

Out of Bounds	Within Bounds	Out of Bounds
Super-nice and accommodating to everyone	Neutral to upbeat, expecting positive outcomes	Sarcastic, cynical, or negative

There's a playing field for every behavior. Once you've come to grips with what is desirable or permissible, like any great athlete, you can choose to play at the edge of the playing field from time to time, but don't go out of bounds too often.

TRUTH 55

SPEAKING WITH IMPACT REQUIRES PAUSE AND PUNCH

Ever wonder why, when some people speak, everyone turns to listen? Or why some people get interrupted more often than others? It's unlikely that the content of what they're saying is particularly boring or interesting. Nor does it have to do with the presence or absence of anything "magical" like charisma. When it comes down to it, it's all about the rhythm: the beat and timing of what they say.

Speaking with impact—making a strong, positive, and memorable impression on your listeners—requires a steady and confident rhythm, not too fast and not too slow. The pauses need to be in the right places, and the emphasis on key words and thoughts. When giving an important talk or speech, you should approach what you say as a

When giving an important talk or speech, approach what you say as a singer would approach a song.

singer would approach a song. The words, or lyrics, are not enough to engage on their own. It is the rhythm, or the accompanying melody, that brings them to life.

Roberta, a native New Yorker, spoke with loads of enthusiasm and energy. During presentations she would hardly pause to breathe. With no way to get a word in edgewise, others would either interrupt her in midstream or would simply tune her out after a while. With no pauses at the ends of sentences or after key words, it was impossible to process what she said.

Philippe, from Montreal, seemed to have the opposite problem. When talking with others, Philippe would trail off after a dozen words. Someone else would then jump in and take over. In a typical meeting, he'd get interrupted several times and found it hard to make his point.

What Roberta and Philippe had in common was a shared solution to their public speaking problems. When each of them, aided by a metronome, started to apply what I call simple "pause and punch" techniques to public speaking, they immediately gained more of their listeners' attention and won more respect over time. Roberta used the metronome to slow down her pace and to practice pausing to count to 3 after sentences. Philippe wrote down what he wanted to cover and stayed on a steady course with the metronome until he reached the end of his thought.

The rhythm of impact has three essential components:

■ **Beat.** Speaking with a steady beat, slow enough to allow you to enunciate carefully and completely, allows others to keep up with what you're saying.

Practicing with a metronome can help you become conscious of your speaking pace.

■ **Pause.** Pausing after each important phrase or word immediately makes it more memorable, because it stands out in the space left by the pause. In the phrase "Ask not what your country can do for you," for example, leaving a slight pause after the "not" emphasizes the negative and draws people's attention to what follows.

■ **Punch.** Giving more "punch" or emphasis to important ideas helps others tune in to remember them. When you complete the famous sentence with "ask what you can do for your country," giving an extra push of air behind the "you" as it leaves your mouth establishes the key point of that message in the minds of your listeners.

Every beat, pause, or punch helps shapes your message. Bear these three elements in mind whenever you need to get your point across. Speaking with impact is one of the best ways to get noticed and be considered for leadership positions.

PART XII

THE TRUTH
ABOUT
MOVING ON

TRUTH 56

GOOD CAREER PLANNING REQUIRES YOU TO KNOW YOURSELF

A young executive named Robert reluctantly went through the General Electric career-planning program: three days of looking at where he wanted to be at what stage of his working life. Rather busy at the time, 24-year-old Robert felt it was a bit early for this kind of thing. However, after completing the assignments, he realized that being in charge of many people meant a lot to him. He determined that his long-term goal was to be the top person in his profession at a major company before he was 50.

When Robert's career started to stall at a major Fortune 50 company, that objective stuck in his mind. He knew he needed to move if he were to make it to his goal. Robert worked for four more companies, expanding his role every time, always considering that endgame. Now almost 60, Robert has reached his goal and beyond. He is president of a major U.S. corporation, running a $30 billion business. He credits that course 36 years ago that helped him become clear about his career goals.

We can all learn something from Robert's clarity of vision. However, it would be a mistake to assume that you share his idea of a successful career and to try to imitate his strategy. It is a workplace myth that most people are ambitious to get ahead—one reinforced by a culture of promotion meaning success. The truth is that different people are motivated by and committed to different things. The best bit of career planning you will ever do is to spend some time getting to know yourself. Then you can focus on what you really want.

> *The best bit of career planning you will ever do is to spend some time getting to know yourself.*

There are four principal ways to find satisfaction at work: to get ahead, to get secure, to get free, and to get high. Which of these, or which combination of these, is most like you?

- **Get-ahead** people enjoy competition, one-upmanship, and risk. They are good at thinking years ahead and are comfortable working with lots of politics.

- **Get-secure** people enjoy being competent at their jobs. They may seem territorial, wanting to become an irreplaceable expert by knowing more about something than others at work, such as legal stuff or finances. They may hate taking vacations since they need to feel irreplaceable.

- **Get-free** people want to be able to do their own thing. They often carve niches in esoteric areas that enable them to pursue personal interests. Roles as consultants or academics can allow them to determine their own working patterns, but they often choose to work for themselves.

- **Get-high** people need to do work that not only matters to them but that they love with a passion. They enjoy being challenged and may be entrepreneurs, researchers, or project leaders.

If it's not immediately clear what resonates as your modus operandi, try drawing up a three-column list of What I Need at Work, What I Want at Work, and What I Don't Want at Work. Include everything that comes to mind, and see what themes and patterns emerge. You then will be in an informed position to look at how opportunities coincide with these themes. Adjust your list every six months or so. As you experience different working situations, you'll get clearer about what you want. And the richer and clearer your vision is, the easier it is to work toward it.

Knowing yourself and knowing where you want to go helps you focus on the bigger picture of your working life and keeps you from getting distracted or discouraged by the small frustrations or slow patches. It also stops you from leaping into the wrong job just because you think you should accept a promotion. It may be that you should stay put, move sideways, or even move on.

TRUTH 57

MOVING UP MEANS LETTING GO

When you move from a position as a star individual player to one where you are responsible for managing many other people, it's a whole new ballgame. The very strengths that got you noticed and helped you move up—super motivation, attention to detail, and strong follow-up—can now trip you up if you try to use them in exactly the same way as before.

Moving into a position of managerial responsibility is one of the most challenging transitions in organizational life. The temptation is to carry on doing what you're good at, alongside your new responsibilities, somehow fitting it all in. This is categorically wrong! You need to let go of former roles and the way you did things before in order to focus on doing the new job well. You also need to let go so that your new staff can focus on getting on with their work, which will include the stuff you used to do. This process may take time—time you don't think you have—but unless you invest time and thought early on to setting up effective working systems and relationships, you will get into bad habits and will never be able to completely move up.

The problem is that the better you are at what you do, the more frustrating you find it to delegate. By the time you've explained to someone how to do something, you might as well have done it yourself! It's hard to believe that other people don't work exactly the way you do and do exactly what's needed without being told. It's also hard to accept that there are other ways of doing things in addition to your own. However, it has to be done.

> *Moving into a position of managerial responsibility is one of the most challenging transitions in organizational life.*

Here are the key strategies for learning how to take your hands off, when starting a new managerial job, while staying hands-on where and when it matters:

- **Lose the perfectionism.** One of the most important things you can do, for yourself and others, is to let go of any perfectionist expectations. They belong in your past.

- **Communicate your expectations.** What you need to do now is set up consistent and reasonable parameters for your staff. Make your standards for competent (not perfect!) performance clear. It can help to give the team examples of good work and formats for any regular reports.

- **Establish clear working relationships.** Clearly define how you want to work with and delegate to your team. They need to be sure how to keep you informed and how you expect them to work with others (internal or external to the team).

- **Take time to explore what works.** In establishing your working relationship with your team, especially if you have never held a similar role, you should let them know that the guidelines will evolve over time as you all get used to working with each other.

- **Take control when necessary.** While you want to avoid overdirecting or controlling your staff and setting too many rules, you also need to be willing to confront poor performance or behavior and to know that your staff will take you seriously when you do. You need to negotiate an effective middle ground between being too lax and too tough.

- **Give clear instructions.** Good delegating means being clear and firm about what you want—specifically, what you want, from whom, and by when. (And also keeping track of that yourself, either via a computer reminder system or with a good old-fashioned pen-and-paper To Do list.)

Letting go while guiding others is a delicate balance to negotiate. It's something you get better at over time. However, with some good planning and consistent follow-up, you can rise to the occasion and ensure a successful future for both you and your team.

TRUTH 58

THE GRASS ISN'T ALWAYS GREENER ON THE OTHER SIDE OF THE FENCE

When the economy heats up, or your enthusiasm for your job cools down, you may start to notice more attractive jobs elsewhere. Perhaps you are lured by the prospect of an attractive salary, great benefits, or an exciting new organizational culture. This is just what the folks thought who joined dot-coms during the Internet boom. However, as many of them found out, some of those attractive new options may turn out to be illusions.

Look before you leap is the motto for anyone thinking about moving on. And don't just look—look hard! Before you move on, you need to be sure that the job is right for you and that you are choosing it for the right reasons. You may look at what other people do and think it looks like easy money but not notice all the background work they have to

Before you move on, you need to be sure that the job is right for you and that you are choosing it for the right reasons.

put in. It may be that you're actually better off sticking with your old job.

Michael, a civil servant, had a degree in education. When a local high school offered him a position as a history teacher, along with a coaching assignment, he was thrilled. Not only did the jobs look easy—he'd taught history before—but together they equaled his current salary. He'd also have lots of time off over the summer. However, when Michael talked with his teacher friends about the job offer, they pointed out things he hadn't considered. He hadn't thought about all the phone calls he would have to make to kids to remind them to come to practice and all the calls he would receive from parents wanting to know why their kid wasn't in the game. Nor had he factored in the time he would spend at every game, including the playoffs at the end of the season. He'd actually be working much longer hours than his current job, and his weekends would be shot. Maybe a bit more time off in the summer didn't really make up for all that. Michael stayed put.

So how do you find out if a new job is right for you?

- **Do your research.** Although you can never really know what a new job will entail until you're doing it, you need to try to get a sense of what goes on behind the scenes. Michael did the right thing by asking friends for advice. If you don't have an immediate contact, you can network to find someone who knows something about the job, or someone at the company.

- **Test the waters.** You can check out an interesting-looking job by interviewing for it and using the interview as a chance to ask questions. But don't forget that in an interview the company is also trying to sell itself to you and may not be entirely honest.

■ **Be sure of your motivations.** You need to be certain of why you want to move. A challenging new job might look exciting and glamorous, but if what you actually want out of working life is ease and security, it's not the job for you. Make a list of your wants and needs from a job, and see how your current and potential positions score against it. You also need to think about what you really don't want, and test the new job description against that.

■ **Weigh the salary and perks.** Don't be dazzled by salary alone. The compensation in a job is the total package offered. This can include bonuses, perks, training and development, retirement plan options, financial planning, and so on as well as salary. And that's just the tangibles. Intangibles include how supportive your new boss is and how much potential there is for career advancement.

While not making wild leaps without forethought into a new position, it's definitely worth keeping an eye on options outside your current job. It's hard to know what's possible for you, and whether it makes sense to move, unless you have something to benchmark against. Then, when you know you have good reason to move on, you'll already have well-thought-out plans in mind.

TRUTH 59

CAREER DERAILMENT CAN HAPPEN AT ANY TIME

You just got a promotion, you have the total support of your boss, and you're playing golf with her boss. Everything looks good! But don't relax too soon. There may be minefields ahead on this wonderful career path.

However successful you are, virtually everyone experiences shaky moments in a career. The irony is, these instances often occur at times when failure seems unlikely, so you are not on the lookout for it. Following a long spell of good results, such as when you're happy with your achievements and respected by others, it doesn't take long for comfort to slip into complacency. Or after a major promotion, when your talent has just been acknowledged and rewarded.

> *Following a long spell of good results, it doesn't take long for comfort to slip into complacency.*

In the case of a promotion, the transition period can bring more trouble than joy if you're not careful. You're taken away from familiar situations and required to adapt to something new. "Winging it" and relying on your memory for follow-up may have worked in a smaller job. Now that you have a bigger job, you may need to develop better work habits to enable you to cope. Also, beware of newfound power in a higher position. It can go to your head so that you think you can do no wrong. Before you know it, the mood can turn, mistakes can be made, and you'll find yourself sidelined into some "specialty" role or, worse, out of a job.

The Center for Creative Leadership uses the term "derailment factors" to describe minefields that appear in the path of previously successful executives. Their research has shown that there are three major reasons for career derailment in the U.S. and Europe:

- **Poor working relations.** Failing to effectively network or build consensus with key stakeholders, or experiencing ongoing conflicts or communication problems with colleagues.

- **Inability to develop or adapt.** Having trouble coming to grips with the way things are done in a new position or workplace.

- **Organizational isolation.** Putting up boundaries around your unit or department, isolating it from the rest of the organization and from external influences.

Malcolm, a superb salesman, suffered from all three. Following a great performance turning around a small team, he was made co-head of sales and marketing, leading 220 people in four offices. The other co-head had great marketing ideas but wasn't very good at sales, so they made a good partnership on paper. Without further ado, Malcolm immediately started visiting all the sales offices, trying to pump up the staff, just as he always had done before with his small team. He didn't stop to consider what the promotion meant, to look at the bigger picture, or to strategize. Spreading himself over more locations, Malcolm began to get overloaded, forgot details, and missed appointments. As people tried to intervene, Malcolm got defensive about his territory and started publicly conflicting with his co-head.

As Malcolm hit minefield after minefield, his former boss started dropping hints. Malcolm didn't pay attention. He thought that if he got his numbers up, everything would be OK. Then, after just three months, management told him they were thinking about replacing him. Given another three months to turn around his performance, Malcolm suddenly opened his eyes to the mess around him. He invested in a coach, who gathered comprehensive feedback from everyone around him in the organization and then worked with him to change his ways.

Don't make the same mistake as Malcolm. When you are in the thick of things, it can be hard to spot that derailment is imminent. But even if you don't notice, you can be sure that others will. Take any feedback very seriously. Once you realize that things are off-kilter, take urgent steps to ask trusted colleagues for more details and advice on the things that aren't working. Then do everything you can to get back on track.

TRUTH 60

WHEN YOU'VE RUN OUT OF REAL ESTATE, IT'S TIME TO MOVE

When your family gets too big for your home, what do you do? Move. In the same way, when your ability grows beyond the boundaries of your current position, it's time to think about a change. It's hard to stay motivated in a job that no longer challenges you. Moving up, or even out, can give you a new lease on your work life.

The right time to consider a move is *before* you get bored, and ideally before you feel you have fully mastered your job. Total mastery is for experts, not for those who want to get ahead. Ambitious people need to constantly push themselves to new challenges. If your "job knowledge" is near zero when you start, the ideal time to start looking is when your mastery is around 70 percent.

> *The right time to consider a move is before you get bored and before you have fully mastered your job.*

This is one situation where if you don't ask, you don't get. Before looking elsewhere, share your aspirations with your company. If they don't want to lose you, they may work to find you a new post, even if nothing is officially open. Be specific in your requests, and give them time. This sort of thing can take some maneuvering. Nevertheless, sometimes it becomes clear that the only way you'll get the next job is to step into your boss's shoes, and he or she is showing no sign of moving. When that's the case, how do you consider your options?

Take the case of Jose, who worked for a large U.S. corporation in Mexico, traveling regularly to ensure manufacturing quality worldwide. Jose was ambitious and knew that he had a lot to offer. He had worked his way up from the factory floor via a degree in supply-chain management. So when his old boss visited Mexico, Jose leaped at the opportunity to have a career discussion. However, as he spelled out his ambitions, his mentor smiled sadly. "Do you really think that with three U.S. peers in the business you have much chance of getting your boss's job?" he said. "And you know there isn't much for you in the company otherwise."

At 32, Jose realized that he might be doing the same job for a very long time. Rather than get frustrated, he sat down to rethink his career, taking the following steps. Anyone in a similar situation should do likewise.

- First, he did an inventory of his "wants, needs, and no-no's." This set out what he desired in a job, what he couldn't live without, and what he wanted to avoid. Jose identified that he wanted to carry on doing something interesting in manufacturing, but that he needed independence and time with his family. He also didn't want to do all that overseas traveling anymore.

- Next, he explored options that would give him what he "needed," meet some of his "wants," and avoid his "no-no's." He weighed finding something else in his company and then looked around outside. His professional society gave him some advice to help with this. Jose decided that owning his own business looked the most promising.

- Finally, he investigated what he would have to do to start a business, checking out what he needed to learn and weighing the pluses and minuses before making any decisions about handing in his notice.

Doing an inventory exercise is a proven and useful way to focus your thoughts. Follow Jose's example whenever you feel hemmed in by your job. Whether you ultimately decide to stay put or move on, running a "reality check" will help keep you on the right path to career success.

REFERENCES

FURTHER READING

Part I: The Truth About Starting a New Job

1. A good text to look at on this topic from a leadership perspective is **Gabarro, John J., *The Dynamics of Taking Charge*, Harvard Business School Press, 1987**. This examines real-life cases of general managers taking up new positions and the factors that made them succeed or fail.

2. On the subject of hitting the ground running, **Watkins, Michael, *The First 90 Days: Critical Success Strategies for New Leaders at All Levels*, Harvard Business School Press, 2003** is better than any of the others on the market. **Watkins, Michael and Ciampa, Dan, *Right from the Start: Taking Charge in a New Leadership Role*, Harvard Business School Press, 1999** also offers useful advice on joining a new organization and effecting change, illustrated by interviews and case studies.

3. I'm not a great fan of the book as a whole, but Chapter/Habit 5 "Seek First to Understand, Then to Be Understood" in **Covey, Stephen R., *The 7 Habits of Highly Effective People*, Free Press, 2004** offers good

insight on the issue of keeping silent when embarking upon a new position in order to learn. (I would also like to thank Tom McLaughlin for this superb advice more than 30 years ago.)

4. **Holton, Ed et al,** *So You're New Again: How to Succeed When You Change Jobs*, **Berrett Koehler Publishers, Inc., 2001** is a useful guide on how to understand and fit in to a new organizational environment and culture, rather than trying to impose your old place's ways upon it.

5. Taking a broader view than just the office or organization, but no less, and possibly more, useful for that reason, the classic **Ardrey, Robert,** *The Territorial Imperative: A Personal Inquiry into the Animal Origins of Property and Nations,* **Dell Pub Co, 1966** looks with great insight into the fundamentals of why we all like our own space. Don't forget that territory matters to all animals, humans included.

6. **Joni, Saj-Nicole,** *The Third Opinion: How Successful Leaders Use Outside Insight to Create Superior Results*, **Portfolio Hardcover, 2004** has a unique perspective on the usefulness of networking, establishing trusted relationships, and using outside advisors in your work. Joni is one of the few writers who deals with using consultants and others to check your thinking and make sure that you have a clear view of what needs to be done.

7. I recommend **Joni, Saj-Nicole,** *The Third Opinion: How Successful Leaders Use Outside Insight to Create Superior Results*, **Portfolio Hardcover, 2004** for this

chapter too, for its discussion of the idea of structural trust and how organizational design can work against that. It's one of few books around that actually looks at whom to trust, rather than making others trust you. Joni's article **"The Geography of Trust,"** *Harvard Business Review*, **March 2004, pp. 82-88**, is also insightful. Additionally, **Bibb, Sally and Kourdi, Jeremy,** *Trust Matters: For Organisational and Personal Success*, **Palgrave Macmillan, 2004** succinctly summarizes the role of trust, and how to build it, in business relationships, while **Galford, Robert M. and Seibold Drapeau, Anne,** *The Trusted Leader*, **Free Press, 2003** go into further detail about other different types of trust: from personal to organizational.

Part II: The Truth About Working with Bosses

8. There is nothing substantial out there that I recommend on the theme of honoring your boss. However, if you want to look at the issue from another perspective, and like a fun read, then try Badowski, **Rosanne and Gittines, Roger,** *Managing Up: How to Forge an Effective Relationship with Those Above You*, **Currency, 2003**. Jack Welch's ex PA, Badowski argues that all of us are in some respect secretaries to our bosses: Our job is to take on their agenda and make their life easier. In return, we get to influence that agenda.

9. **Katz, Steven L.,** *Lion Taming: Working Successfully with Leaders, Bosses, and Other Tough Customers,*

Sourcebooks, 2004, written by a former advisor to four U.S. senators, offers an interesting take on the impact that bosses have on our reputations. Characterizing leaders as lions, Katz offers tips on how to manage and maneuver these characters into a working relationship that brings both of you success. **Jay, Ros, *How to Manage Your Boss: Or Colleagues, or Anybody Else You Need to Develop a Good and Profitable Relationship With*, Prentice Hall, 2002** takes a more everyday approach to developing the kind of working relationship with your boss that results in maximum benefit for you.

10. **Culbert, Samuel A., and Ullmen, John B., *Don't Kill the Bosses!: Escaping the Hierarchy Trap*, Berrett-Koehler, 2001** is insightful on hierarchy at work. It paints a clear picture of the different ways that hierarchy operates in the workplace, suggesting approaches to improve your relationships with all colleagues, not just bosses.

11. There are many books out there addressing the topic of unsatisfactory or unpleasant bosses. Two interesting ones are **Lubit, Roy H., *Coping with Toxic Managers, Subordinates …And Other Difficult People: Using Emotional Intelligence to Survive and Prosper*, Financial Times Prentice Hall, 2003**, which looks at behaviors of five distinct types of difficult managers and how one should respond to them, and **Sharpe, Davida and Johnson, Elinor, *Managing Conflict with Your Boss*, CCL Press, 2002** with its useful steps to moving your relationship with your boss in a more productive direction.

Part III: The Truth About Working with Others

12. The field of emotional intelligence (EI) offers useful insight into the challenges of working with others. A strong basic text looking at the issues from an organizational perspective is **Weisinger, Hendrie, *Emotional Intelligence at Work*, Jossey-Bass, 2000**. It shows how to develop your EI to improve both self-awareness and communication with others. Weisinger's advice is backed by both personal experience and solid research.

13. The theory of transactional analysis—a type of psychotherapy based on the understanding of interactions between ourselves and others—helps with thinking about goodwill at work. Where better to start than with the man who coined the term: **Berne, Eric, *Games People Play: The Basic Handbook of Transactional Analysis*, Ballantine Books, 1996** (republished) is one of the most influential and popular psychology books ever published; it shows how good relationships are based upon positive exchanges. Additionally, try **Acuff, Jerry and Wood, Wally, *The Relationship Edge in Business: Connecting with Customers and Colleagues When It Counts*, John Wiley and Sons, 2004**, which offers a great example of advance bank account filling through your approach to and treatment of others, as you sow goodwill in your encounters.

14. Diversity is a hot topic in corporate life and there are many texts to choose from. Better ones include **Billings-Harris, Lenora, *The Diversity Advantage: A Guide to Making Diversity Work*, OakHill Press, 1998**, which offers a

simple and effective introduction to the subject through question-based chapters on key issues for the American workforce; *Harvard Business Review on Managing Diversity*, **Harvard Business School Press, 2002**, a collection of strong articles addressing diversity from many perspectives; and **Miller, Frederick A. et al,** *The Inclusion Breakthrough*, **Berrett-Koehler Publishers, 2002**. This last book broadens the issue of diversity to look at more than workforce make-up, considering the whole organizational culture's attitude toward difference, and showing how belief in diversity can lead to stronger results for everyone. Finally, if you want something very practical about working with people from different cultural backgrounds, try **Chaney, Lillian H., and Martin, Jeanette S.,** *Intercultural Business Communication, Third Edition*, **Prentice Hall, 2003**. Diversity and inclusion issues are not necessarily the same elsewhere as they are in the U.S.

15. For those committed to becoming better listeners, **Burley-Allen, Madelyn,** *Listening: The Forgotten Skill: A Self-Teaching Guide*, **Wiley Self-Teaching Guides, 1995** is a classic practical program for tuning your active listening abilities. Highly recommended. If you're interested in learning more about the different ways in which people listen, or don't listen, to each other, and the implications for relationships, particularly between men and women, try **Tannen, Deborah,** *You Just Don't Understand*, **Ballantine Books, 1991**. If you want to think about how to improve listening in general in your organization, I

suggest **Kline, Nancy,** *Time to Think: Listening to Ignite the Human Mind,* **Cassell Illustrated, 1998,** which shows how to put the power of effective listening to use to generate a more open and innovative workplace.

16. When it comes to giving out criticism, **Haden Elgin, Suzette,** *How to Disagree Without Being Disagreeable: Getting Your Point Across with the Gentle Art of Verbal Self-Defense,* **Wiley, 1997** and **Haden Elgin, Suzette,** *The Gentle Art of Verbal Self-Defense at Work,* **Prentice Hall Press, 2000** are classic guides to keeping the temperature down during difficult exchanges. The more recent book takes you through different possible workplace confrontations and how to deal with them, and is more relevant to an executive, helping you understand what pushes others' buttons. Less directly relevant to work, but the granddaddy of all books on tough conversations is **Stone, Douglas et al,** *Difficult Conversations: How to Discuss What Matters Most,* **Penguin Putnam, 2000.** The "feelings" stuff may fall a bit flat at work, but it effectively shows how not to leave others with bruised feelings while retaining control of the conversation. Then there is the classic **Carnegie, Dale,** *How to Win Friends & Influence People,* **Pocket, 1990,** which is mentioned in the chapter.

17. There is nothing I would specifically recommend on getting to meetings on time. Just do it! If you need reminders, get someone else to help you. That's all there is to it. But for advice on how to ensure that your own meetings start and end promptly, and don't knock other people's timing off,

I suggest **Hawkins, Charlie,** *First Aid for Meetings: Quick Fixes and Major Repairs for Running Effective Meetings*, **Bookpartners, 1997**. The classic **Doyle, Michael,** *How to Make Meetings Work*, **Jove Books, 1993** is a very good basic, taking you through the factors that make a meeting productive or not.

18. I have searched long and hard for something on confidentiality at work that goes beyond practical information/knowledge management or legal advice, and never found anything. There is plenty on how to facilitate information flow, and open up the movement of knowledge throughout the organization, but little on how to restrict it, or on the need to be aware of the trouble it can cause. Do let me know if you find anything! However, if you are interested in the processes by which information flows around an organization, and the positives of that, one of the most interesting books on the market is **Cross, Rob et al,** *The Hidden Power of Social Networks: Understanding How Work Really Gets Done in Organizations*, **Harvard Business School Press, 2004**. It offers guidance on how to get the information that you want through collaboration with others.

Part IV: The Truth About Networking

19. An important book that gets you thinking about the role the networker plays in organizational life, and a good one for thinking about networking in general is **Gladwell,**

Malcolm, *The Tipping Point: How Little Things Can Make a Big Difference*, **Back Bay Books, 2002**. Gladwell illustrates, among other things, the power of the "connector" in generating a tipping point: the moment when something unique or unusual becomes common and popular. Napier Collyns, whom I mention in Truth 17, is one such connector.

20. If you are new to networking, or a bit of an introvert, there are good books out there to help you with the basics of starting, and maintaining, a conversation. For example, **RoAne, Susan, *How to Work a Room: The Ultimate Guide to Savvy Socializing in Person and Online*, HarperResource, 2000**. Another general but popular guide to the wider art of networking is **Nierenberg, Andrea R., *Nonstop Networking: How to Improve Your Life, Luck, and Career*, Capital Books (VA), 2002**. For specific useful advice on creating your quick introduction and 30-second elevator speech, try **Fisher, Donna, *People Power: How to Create a Lifetime Network for Business, Career, and Personal Advancement*, Bard Press, 1995**.

21. I haven't ever found much directly covering the issues of polling or asking for opinions at work. However, if you are interested in thinking about the issue from a big-picture point of view, **Surowiecki, James, *The Wisdom of Crowds: Why the Many Are Smarter Than the Few and How Collective Wisdom Shapes Business, Economies, Societies and Nations*, Doubleday, 2004** has good guidance on the importance of polling diverse

populations or people. There are also some interesting books on consensus and collaboration on the market. They are helpful as one way to put polling skills to work. I suggest **Straus, David and Layton, Thomas C.,** *How to Make Collaboration Work: Powerful Ways to Build Consensus, Solve Problems, and Make Decisions,* **Berrett-Koehler 2002**, with its five tested principles of collaboration.

22. For good background to Stanley Milgram and his work, try **Blass, Thomas,** *The Man Who Shocked the World: The Life and Legacy of Stanley Milgram,* **Basic Books, 2004**. A comprehensive biography of Milgram, this goes into detail about his experiments. If you are a novice networker and would like to think a bit more about how this theory can serve you, try **Darling, Diane,** *The Networking Survival Guide: Get the Success You Want By Tapping Into the People You Know,* **McGraw-Hill, 2003**. However, this is very basic, and not for someone who already has a strong network or who networks naturally.

23. When thinking about how to discover and generate commonalities for the purposes of network-building, I find **Mackay, Harvey,** *Dig Your Well Before You're Thirsty: The Only Networking Book You'll Ever Need,* **Currency, 1999** helpful. This shows you how to get the most out of all the relationships that you already have, as well as tips on doing advance research for people you have yet to forge a link with.

24. **Carducci, Bernardo J.,** *The Pocket Guide to Making Successful Small Talk: How to Talk to Anyone Anytime Anywhere About Anything,* **Pocket Guide Company, 1999** is a good primer and reference on social chat. With the message that social talk is an acquired skill, not an innate ability, it sets out the golden rules and offers advice for specific situations. The same author comes at the subject from a different direction in **Carducci, Bernardo J., and Golant, Susan,** *Shyness: A Bold New Approach,* **Perennial Currents, 2000**. Not just for the shy, the book asserts that most of us suffer from some form of shyness at some point in our lives, and offers diverse techniques for coping with specific workplace situations.

Part V: The Truth About Getting Things Done

25. There are many books about closing the sale. However, most are targeted at actual salespeople, rather than offering advice on the selling of ideas, opinions, and projects for people of all job descriptions. An exception is **Maurer, Rick,** *Why Don't You Want What I Want? How to Win Support for Your Ideas Without Hard Sell, Manipulation, or Power Plays,* **Bard Press, 2002**, which takes you through six principles of engagement to arrive at desired outcomes, without treading on others' opinions. A more classic yet still useful sales book is **Denny, Richard,** *Selling to Win: Tested Techniques for Closing the Sale,* **Kogan Page, 1988**. This bestseller

stresses that successful selling is achieved through building long-term relationships, not quick hard pushes.

26. When it comes to conveying the bottom line effectively, I can't find anything to beat **Minto, Barbara, *The Pyramid Principle: Logic in Writing and Thinking*, Pitman Publishing, 1995**. This shows how to structure clear and orderly communication to really get your message across and help people move toward shared goals. It is the basis for the work of most consulting organizations and MBA programs worldwide. A great book but not a quick read. Looking at clear communication from another perspective—how to cope with the complexity outside yourself as opposed to that in your mind—try **Bushe, Gervase, *Clear Leadership: How Outstanding Leaders Make Themselves Understood, Cut Through the Mush, and Help Everyone Get Real at Work*, Davis-Black Publishing, 2001**. It provides advice not only on how to communicate clearly, but on how to help others have confidence in their own opinions and communication abilities.

27. Bouncing back from adversity is not easy, and in the end it's down to personal strength and experience more than following tips from a book. Nonetheless, **Maddi, Salvatore and Khoshaba, Deborah M., *Resilience at Work: How to Succeed No Matter What Life Throws at You*, American Management Association, 2005** offers effective techniques for building what they define as the core hardiness attitudes for coping with difficulty at work: commitment, control, and challenge. For a more

direct and humorous non-business take on the subject, I recommend **Carville, James and Begala, Paul, *Buck Up, Suck Up . . . and Come Back When You Foul Up: 12 Winning Secrets from the War Room*, Simon & Schuster, 2003.** Two top political consultants apply political lessons to the business world. It's candid and real, but some political persuasions might find it a bit tough, since the authors wear their politics on their sleeves!

28. There is little or nothing out there looking at relationships between managers and support staff in any depth. However, if you're searching for ways to reward and acknowledge support staff in the manner discussed in the chapter, you may find texts on staff motivation offer ideas or inspiration. **Ventrice, Cindy, *Make Their Day! Employee Recognition That Works*, Berrett-Koehler, 2003** places emphasis on good working relationships as the key to effective staff recognition, while **Bruce, Anne and Pepitone, James S., *Motivating Employees*, McGraw-Hill, 1998** offers case histories of how different organizations have addressed the issue of encouraging and rewarding staff.

Part VI: The Truth About Managing Your Workload

29. Some of the many time-management books on the market can be helpful with prioritizing. **Morgenstern, Julie, *Making Work Work: New Strategies for Surviving and Thriving at the Office*, Fireside, 2004**, with its four Ds (delete, delay, delegate and diminish) has been found helpful

by many. I also recommend **Koch, Richard, *The 80/20 Principle: The Secret to Success by Achieving More with Less*, Currency, 1999**. Koch helps the reader work out which 20 percent of activity will bring the best returns, stressing the principle of focus.

30. **Smith, Manuel J., *When I Say No I Feel Guilty, Vol. II, for Managers and Executives*, A Train Pr, 2000**) is the classic on assertiveness and, as the title says, helps equip readers with the confidence and the strategies to say No at work and make their own needs known. Also useful, although not addressing the issue from a specifically workplace perspective, is **Braiker, Harriet, *The Disease to Please*, McGraw-Hill, 2002**. This bestseller offers a set of principles and a 21-Day Action Plan to help the reader reduce the urge to comply without regard to personal and professional consequences.

31. The setting of clear boundaries at work by a team member rather than the delegating leader is another topic where it's hard to find a really useful text. However, **Avery, Christopher M. at al, *Teamwork Is an Individual Skill: Getting Your Work Done When Sharing Responsibility*, Berrett-Koehler, 2001**, while placing the focus on fulfilling your own responsibility as a team member, emphasizes that part of that is about pulling others up when they don't pull their weight or shift ground rules, with practical advice on how to deal with that. **Schechter, Harriet, *Conquering Chaos at Work: Strategies for Managing Disorganization and the People Who Cause***

It, **Fireside, 2000** offers a humorous take on how to stop fuzzy boundaries and carelessness of others at work having detrimental effects on your own achievements.

32. Which are the good practical books to help you get to grips with organizing paper, files, and reports? This is another topic where there's a lot available, but not all of it offers advice that is really useful and applicable to today's workplace. One recent exception that many people have found useful is **Hemphill, Barbara, *Taming the Paper Tiger at Work*, Kiplinger Books, 2002**, which acknowledges that despite new communication methods, we still deal with as much paper as ever.

33. Project management guides often contain useful advice on how to set, manage and meet deadlines amid the complexity of organizational life. **Tobis, Michael and Tobis, Irene, *Managing Multiple Projects*, McGraw-Hill, 2002**, stress reliability as one of the most important qualities you can offer an organization. They help the reader to develop a reliable system for managing workload, weighing up time against quality. More basic and functional, but useful for those starting out, is **Williams, Paul, *Getting a Project Done on Time: Managing People, Time, and Results*, American Management Association, 1996**. It shows you how to manage and work with others to ensure that projects are delivered on time.

Part VII: The Truth About Getting Your Point Across

34. McLuhan, as the chapter says, is the granddaddy of the concept that the medium is the message. Two good introductions to his work are **McLuhan, Marshall and Fiore, Quentin, *The Medium Is the Message*, Gingko Press, 2005**, which effectively condenses his ideas in innovative graphic form and **McLuhan, Eric and Zingrone, Frank (eds.), *Essential McLuhan*, Basic Books, 1996**, a collection of articles from his key texts. As for developing greater understanding of the communication preferences discussed in this chapter, you'll find the field of NLP (neuro-linguistic programming) will give you perspective on how you relate to and read other people, and help improve your communication skills. A good general introduction is **O'Connor, Joseph and Seymour, John, *Introducing Neuro-Linguistic Programming: Psychological Skills for Understanding and Influencing People*, Thorsons Publishers, 1993**. For the most useful scoop on how the brain works to influence communication, the place to look is **Markova, Dawna, *The Art of the Possible: A Compassionate Approach to Understanding the Way People Think, Learn and Communicate*, Conari Press, 1991**. This book shows you how to identify your own ways of processing information, as well as those of other people with whom you communicate.

35. Presentation skills books are the best source of advice on effective introductions and conclusions to work communications. A great example is **Weissman, Jerry,**

Presenting to Win: The Art of Telling Your Story, **FT Prentice Hall, 2003**. It shows how to capture your audience, and then keep them there, through telling a story that the listener wants to follow. See also **Diresta, Diane,** *Knockout Presentations: How to Deliver Your Message with Power, Punch, and Pizzazz*, **Chandler House Press, 1998**, which takes you through every aspect of delivering an effective presentation, with a very useful section on answering difficult questions. Finally, a classic is **Boettinger, Henry M.,** *Moving Mountains: Or, the Art and Craft of Letting Others See Things Your Way*, **Collier Books, 1974**. The advice on the components of a good presentation is still valid 30 years after first publication.

36. Linguistics professor George Lakoff is the authority on framing your message to achieve the desired response. He doesn't write on workplace issues, but **Lakoff, George,** *Don't Think of an Elephant: Know Your Values and Frame the Debate—The Essential Guide for Progressives*, **Chelsea Green Publishing Company, 2004** is a fascinating look at the way the U.S. political Right and Left position their arguments. It really gets you thinking about how framing works. The classic **Lakoff, George and Johnson, Mark,** *Metaphors We Live By*, **University of Chicago Press, 2003** offers a different perspective on how your choice of language affects the way in which people respond to you. There are also a number of good books with advice on using stories to help you convey your ideas and get people on board. I like

Simmons, Annette, *The Story Factor: Inspiration, Influence, and Persuasion Through the Art of Storytelling*, Perseus Books, 2002 and Allan, Julie, Fairtlough, Gerard and Heinzen, Barbara, *The Power of the Tale: Using Narratives for Organisational Success*, John Wiley and Sons, 2002, which includes a chapter on using scenario stories to help executives imagine the future.

37. When it comes to handling difficult questions, I like the approach in Weissman, Jerry, *In the Line of Fire: How to Handle Tough Questions...When It Counts*, Prentice Hall, 2005. Highly recommended, this text shows you how to deal with every aspect of a hostile or tough exchange, with concrete advice and techniques on how to handle the various questions that may come your way.

38. There's not much available focusing specifically on how to make a good impression at meetings, but there are plenty of books on how to run an effective meeting, and many tips are transferable to the goal of this chapter. I mention Doyle, Michael, *How to Make Meetings Work*, Jove Books, 1993 elsewhere in these references, with good reason. It's a classic on getting the most out of a meeting situation. Another book, with a slightly different take, is Frank, Milo O., *How to Get Your Point Across in 30 Seconds or Less*, Pocket, 1990—useful advice when there are a dozen others all wanting to pitch in! It's a step-by-step guide to building a 30-second message about any issue, which also works on conference-call meetings.

39. Authors and editors have been quick to respond to the rapid rise of e-mail as a primary mode of organizational communication, and many books of advice have been published. If you are serious about upping your e-mailing skills, I suggest **Cavanagh, Christina, *Managing Your E-Mail: Thinking Outside the Inbox*, John Wiley and Sons, 2003** with its focus on not letting e-mail take over your life, and **Booher, Dianna, *E-Writing: 21st Century Tools for Effective Communication*, Pocket 2001**, which offers advice on good writing to help you with all business communication, not just e-mail.

Part VIII: The Truth About Dealing with Enemies and Antibodies

40. When considering the impact of your energy and emotions on others at work, the writing of Hendrie Weisinger is invaluable. In **Weisinger, Hendrie, *Emotional Intelligence at Work*, Jossey-Bass, 1997** he offers a compendium of mind and body techniques to deal with the adrenalin that can impact negatively on your colleagues. It's a solid reference work based on his experiences of controlling his own anger. Hank also wrote another classic, **Weisinger, Hendrie, *Anger at Work: Learning the Art of Anger Management on the Job*, Quill, 1996**. More of a student textbook, but nonetheless comprehensive and engaging is **Fineman, Stephen, *Understanding Emotion at Work*, SAGE Publications, 2003**. This

looks at the many ways in which emotions play out in the workplace, to both negative and positive effect.

41. If you're interested in further advice on not letting difficult or aggressive people get to you, and managing your emotional response, I recommend **Bernstein, Albert J., *Dinosaur Brains: Dealing with All THOSE Impossible People at Work*, Ballantine Books, 1996**. It's a light-hearted but thorough look at the issues. Developing that theme, **Gladwell, Malcolm, *Blink: The Power of Thinking Without Thinking*, Little, Brown, 2005** is also helpful, encouraging you to use your instincts to sense when someone is going to cause you trouble. We "get" a lot at a very primitive level. Also helpful is **Namie, Gary and Namie, Ruth, *The Bully at Work: What You Can Do to Stop the Hurt and Reclaim Your Dignity on the Job*, Sourcebooks, 2000.**

42. **Frankel, Lois P., *Nice Girls Don't Get the Corner Office: 101 Unconscious Mistakes Women Make That Sabotage Their Careers*, Warner Business Books, 2004** puts the big and little things that will hurt your career into perspective, including explaining and complaining. An easy yet informative read. If you find that your tendency to do either thing is getting in your way at work, you might find **Tamm, James W. and Luyet, Ronald J., *Radical Collaboration: Five Essential Skills to Overcome Defensiveness and Build Successful Relationships*, HarperBusiness, 2004** helpful.

43. The classic easy-read text on positive thinking has to be **Carnegie, Dale, *How to Win Friends & Influence***

People, **Pocket, 1990**. Less well known, but no less of a classic is **Ellis, Albert, *A Guide to Rational Living*, Wilshire Book Company, 1975**. The father of cognitive therapy shows you how to change stuck records in your head, and think of your life from a more positive perspective. Recent offerings include the entertaining **Hellman, Paul, *Naked at Work (and Other Fears): How to Stay Sane When Your Job Drives You Crazy*, New American Library, 2002**, which suggests new perspectives on over 100 workplace niggles and anxieties, and **Topchik, Gary S., *Managing Workplace Negativity*, American Management Association, 2000,** which helps you deal with others' negativity as well as your own.

44. For more advice on how to generate the relaxed stress-free mindset essential to a Teflon temperament, I recommend further reading on stress-busters and relaxation techniques to find some that work for you. Try **Davis, Martha et al, *The Relaxation & Stress Reduction Workbook*, New Harbinger Publications, 2000**. It offers a thorough look at the different ways that stress manifests itself, and plenty of good advice on reducing it through means physical and psychological.

Part IX: The Truth About Making the Right Impression

45. It can be hard to work out which of the multiple books currently available on a "dress for success" theme are useful. Many are superficial in their advice. The three that

I recommend here all address the theme of dressing "down" or casually—an often confusing style—as well as looking professional at work. Most jobs these days will require both. I suggest **Bixler, Susan and Nix-Rice, Nancy, *The New Professional Image: From Business Casual to the Ultimate Power Look*, Adams Media Corporation, 1997** as a comprehensive guide to making a good impression; **Maysonaye, Sherry, *Casual Power: How to Power Up Your Nonverbal Communication & Dress Down for Success*, Bright Books, 1999**, which shows how to dress down without losing the respect of others, and **Thourlby, William, *You Are What You Wear (Business and Casual Style in a 'Clicks and Mortar' World)*, Forbes/Wittenburg and Brown, 1995**, with lessons on "visual perception" drawn from Hollywood.

46. A book that I come back to time and time again is **Ailes, Roger, *You Are The Message: Secrets of the Master Communicators*, Irwin Professional Pub, 1987**, with its emphasis on the strong first impressions made by what you say and how you say it. It's a frank practical guide. Likewise, **Toogood, Granville N., *The Articulate Executive: Learn to Look, Act, and Sound Like a Leader*, McGraw-Hill, 1995**, focused around speeches or presentations, offers strong advice on every aspect of how you verbally present yourself to others as confident and in control. Taking a slightly different tack is **Singal, V.J., and Graham, Thomas, *The Articulate Professional*, Sequoia Career Resources, 1993**.

Particularly useful for non-native English speakers, this reference tool of powerful words and phrases can help you build a vocabulary to engage and inspire others. If your vocabulary is not a problem, but your speaking voice lacks gravitas or volume, try **Grant-Williams, Renee,** *Voice Power: Using Your Voice to Captivate, Persuade, and Command Attention*, **American Management Association, 2002**. Physical exercises and actionable advice help you with everything from public speaking to voicemail messages.

47. For practical help with showing staff and others the respect they deserve, look at **Glanz, Barbara,** *Handle with CARE: Motivating and Retaining Employees*, **McGraw-Hill, 2002** or **Bruce Gandy, Dottie,** *30 Days to a Happy Employee: How a Simple Program of Acknowledgment Can Build Trust and Loyalty at Work*, **Fireside, 2001**. The former, based on research with 1000+ employees, offers dozens of examples of how to show empathy and communicate respect through your actions, while the second offers a course in improving relationships through developing a "habit of acknowledgement."

48. Starting a new job is the major "entrance" in working life. Do look at the books I recommend for Truth 1 for tips on how to maximize the impact that you make on others at that time. Additional advice on how a new group of colleagues or staff may perceive you during those vital first days or weeks is found in **Demarais, Ann and White, Valerie,** *First Impressions: What You Don't Know*

About How Others See You, **Bantam, 2004**. Written by two psychologists, this goes beyond superficial perceptions to look at how others perceive your character and intentions during initial interactions, and how you forge connections with them.

49. You won't find much on the shelves that will give you direct guidance on how to "brand" workspace. However, as the chapter says, a clutter-free desktop is a key step toward creating a presence that radiates professionalism. Many people with messy offices don't want help but sometimes need it. Books such as **Kendall-Tacket, Kathleen,** *The Well-Ordered Office: How to Create an Efficient and Serene Workspace*, **New Harbinger Publications, 2005** look at the fundamental reasons why people's desks get out of control, and help you stop things getting that way.

Part X: The Truth About Getting Noticed

50. There are other chapters in this book that look at presentations from other perspectives. I recommend the books listed for **Truth 32** again here. In addition, take a look at **Stevenson, Douglas,** *Never Be Boring Again: Make Your Business Presentations Capture Attention, Inspire Action and Produce Results*, **Cornelia Press, 2004**, which looks at how the judicious use of stories can help you craft presentations to capture an audience. **Campbell, Michael G.,** *Bulletproof Presentations*, **Career Press, 2002**, offers a very straightforward

blueprint to putting together a presentation, with as much focus on content as on structure and mode of delivery.

51. The concept of branding is really "big" at the moment, and many writers and consultants have tried to apply the language and strategy of product and corporate branding to individuals. Two contrasting approaches are summed up by **Andrusia, David, and Haskins, Rick,** *Brand Yourself: How to Create an Identity for a Brilliant Career*, **Ballantine Books, 2000** and **McNally, David and Speak, Karl,** *Be Your Own Brand: A Breakthrough Formula for Standing Out from the Crowd*, **Berrett-Koehler Publishers, 2002**. Andrusia and Haskins focus on the individual as a product, with guidance on how to present and pitch yourself just as you would a new soap, while McNally and Speak take a softer approach, framing the brand as an honest and sincere relationship with others. I find them both interesting. Women, in particular, due to cultural factors, may find the idea of "selling" themselves challenging. I recommend **Fisher Roffer, Robin,** *Make a Name for Yourself : Eight Steps Every Woman Needs to Create a Personal Brand Strategy for Success*, **Broadway, 2002** as encouragement for anyone to whom self-marketing does not come naturally.

52. Business people can learn a lot from actors when looking to make a more powerful impression. Actors learn how to use posture, movement, and voice to project themselves and their role to audiences of all sizes. One book that picks up on this theme is **Halpern, Belle Linda and Lubar,**

Kathy, *Leadership Presence: Dramatic Techniques to Reach Out, Motivate, and Inspire*, **Gotham Books, 2003**. Another good guide to understanding and improving body language is **Lewis, David,** *The Secret Language of Success: Using Body Language to Get What You Want*, **BBS Publishing Corporation, 1995**, which guides the reader on how to project a successful self-image and master the art of "impression management." If you're interested in the bigger issues—how people's self-perception and the impressions they generate are affected by social and organizational factors—I recommend the work of Richard Sennett. Particularly, **Sennett, Richard with Cobb, Jonathan,** *The Hidden Injuries of Class*, **W.W. Norton and Company, 1993)** and **Sennett, Richard,** *Respect in a World of Inequality*, **W. W. Norton and Company, 2004**.

53. For advice on writing that really gets your message across, **Blake, Gary and Bly, Robert W.,** *The Elements of Business Writing: A Guide to Writing Clear, Concise Letters, Memos, Reports, Proposals, and Other Business Documents*, **Longman, 1992** is useful, offering fundamental principles that will help you ensure that every kind of business document you produce communicates clear and strong. **Ditto, Davidson, Wilma,** *Business Writing: What Works, What Won't*, **St. Martin's Griffin, 2001**, a textbook on good business writing that offers advice for clear communications even with the newest technology. Once you've got the basics, the approach of **Lanham, Richard,** *Revising Business*

Prose, **Longman, 1999**, is powerful. This text focuses on honing your initial ideas and words into clear, concise and simple messages, however complex the idea. A unique and essential take on the challenge.

Part XI: The Truth About Getting Ahead

54. When thinking carefully about your position in the company or workforce, **Schein, Edgar H.,** *Career Survival: Strategic Job and Role Planning,* **Pfeiffer, 1994** can help you understand how your work role is defined, how it evolves, and how to ensure that you evolve with it. For an easier and more directly practical read, try **Templar, Richard,** *The Rules of Work: The Unspoken Truth About Getting Ahead in Business,* **Prentice Hall, 2005**, which stresses that being good at your job is not enough if you want to succeed; you need to think strategically about how to get noticed and get ahead.

55. The "feel-good" factor is something that's not really talked about in business books, but to my mind is vital to consider. You can't just go out and buy a book on it, but **Carville, James and Begala, Paul,** *Buck Up, Suck Up . . . and Come Back When You Foul Up: 12 Winning Secrets from the War Room,* **Simon & Schuster, 2003,** offer a frank and gutsy take on "sucking up" from the political perspective, with lessons transferable to the business world.

56. The classic on likeability, summed up by its title, is **Carnegie, Dale,** *How to Win Friends & Influence People,* **Pocket, 1990**. I would also recommend, **Lustberg, Arch,** *How to Sell Yourself: Winning Techniques for Selling Yourself...Your Ideas...Your Message,* **Career Press, 2002**, which frames "likeability" as the secret of successful communication, offering tips on how to use your face, voice, and body to good effect.

57. Women often find it harder to get to grips with the idea of work being a game than men do, so my recommendation here is specifically targeted at them, although relevant to anyone without a sporting background. **Lehan Harragan, Betty,** *Games Your Mother Never Taught You: Corporate Gamesmanship for Women,* **Warner Books, 1981**, helps women understand that work is a game that boys learn to play when they're young. Although gender equality has moved on considerably since this book was first published, the fundamental issues are still the same.

58. **Leeds, Dorothy,** *PowerSpeak: Engage, Inspire, and Stimulate Your Audience,* **Career Press, 2003**, is the best thing on the market on this score, but does tend to focus on presentations and speeches rather than everyday speaking situations. Better on that particular front, and with lots of practical tips and exercises for becoming a more impressive speaker is **Stuttard, Marie,** *The Power of Speech,* **Barron's Educational Series, 1997**.

Part XII: The Truth About Moving On

59. Many of the ideas in this chapter come from **Derr, Clyde Brooklyn,** *Managing the New Careerists: The Diverse Career Success Orientations of Today's Workers,* **Proquest Info and Learning, 1986**. This is a very accessible title. Another text that offers you a set of hooks through which to understand yourself and your career motivation is the classic **Schein, Edgar,** *Career Anchors, Discovering Your Real Values,* **Pfeiffer, 1985** by the granddaddy of career research and thinking. For a more academic approach, I recommend **Mirvis, Philip and Hall, Douglas T.,** "**Psychological success and the boundaryless career,**" **Journal of Organizational Behaviour 15: 365–380** and **Hall, Douglas T.,** *Careers In and Out of Organizations (Foundations for Organizational Science),* **SAGE Publications, 2001,** for its overview of how careers are changing in the modern world and the different approaches currently being taken to career decision-making.

60. My recommendations for how to approach this common but nonetheless daunting challenge of job change include **Betof, Edward H.,** *Just Promoted!: How to Survive and Thrive in Your First 12 Months As a Manager,* **McGraw-Hill, 1992,** which really primes you on how to negotiate organizational power-play and politics, and **Hill, Linda A.,** *Becoming a Manager: How New Managers Master the Challenges of Leadership,* **Harvard Business School Press, 2003**—indispensable advice culled from in-depth research and interviewing of 19 new

managers. **Belker, Loren B.,** *The First-Time Manager*, **American Management Association, 1997** is also helpful, with a comprehensive approach to the challenges you will meet in a position of managerial responsibility, and how to rise to them.

61. **Chambers, Harry E.,** *Getting Promoted: Real Strategies for Advancing Your Career*, **Perseus Books Groups, 1999** is wise on this subject. Chambers stresses that the path to career fulfillment does not necessarily mean actively looking for promotion. You should concentrate on squeezing every drop of learning and experience possible out of the position that you're in to achieve real and sustainable career growth. That way, promotion will look for you when you are ready for it.

62. The concepts of career derailment summarized in this part are best articulated by the Center for Creative Leadership itself. Three good references are **Lombardo, Michael, M.,** *Preventing Derailment: What to Do Before It's Too Late*, **CCL Press, 1989; Chappelow, Craig and Brittain Leslie, Jean,** *Keeping Your Career on Track: Twenty Success Strategies*, **CCL Press, 2000**; and, from a less personal perspective, **Brittain Leslie, Jean and Van Velsor,** *A Look at Derailment Today: North America and Europe*, **CCL Press, 1996**, comparing derailment and success themes over time and across cultures. For some good case histories of derailment, see **McCall, Jr., Morgan W.,** *High Flyers: Developing the Next Generation of Leaders*, **Harvard Business School Press, 1998**.

63. When it comes to moving on, there is helpful advice out there on getting your thoughts and strategy in order, wherever you are in your career. Two that seem particularly helpful for those mid-career are **Wood, Orrin,** *The Executive Job Search: A Comprehensive Handbook for Seasoned Professionals*, **McGraw-Hill, 2003** with plenty of practical advice to help you identify and secure a next step that is right for you, from the very moment that you start thinking about departure. And **Lucht, John,** *Rites of Passage at $100,000 +: The Insider's Lifetime Guide to Executive Job-Changing and Faster Career Progress*, **Viceroy Press, 2001**, offering a frank recruiter's perspective on how to carry out a job hunt and maximize your chances of securing a satisfying and influential position.

The Truth About Getting Your Point Across
...and Nothing But the Truth

BY LONNIE PACELLI

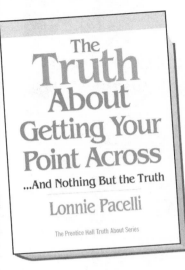

The Truth About Getting Your Point Across will help you communicate more powerfully in any situation: with executives, peers, subordinates, customers, partners, investors, or anyone else. Lonnie Pacelli presents world-class tips and techniques for every communication scenario: meetings, interviews, presentations, team leadership, brainstorming sessions, even elevator pitches. Need to gain credibility with your CEO? Provide better feedback? Motivate teams more effectively? Solve problems more rapidly? Whatever your communication challenge, this book offers proven, fast-access solutions!

ISBN 0131873717, © 2006, 272 pp., $18.99

PUBLISHING IN 2007

The Truth About Being an Effective Leader
...and Nothing But the Truth

BY KAREN OTAZO

Leadership isn't just another step in your career; it's a leap across the great divide. In this book, you'll be learning from the real-life challenges and successes of those who have made the leap. For more than two decades Dr. Otazo has worked with hundreds of leaders worldwide. Her approach gives you necessary guidance to get through the hard work and sticky situations in 52 short, to-the-point chapters that you can shuffle like a deck of cards and use as you need them. You'll learn to steer past the pitfalls and through each challenge as you make the transition to becoming the most effective leader possible.

ISBN 0131873385, © 2007, 208 pp., $18.99